Get Over Yourself

Pray like Your Life Depends on It
(because It Does)
Andi Rispens

Contents

To the women in my life who point me to Christ. This is my attempt to do the same for you.

believe

decide

seek

pray

live

praise

share

Introduction

"THE ANSWER TO A poor prayer life is not to pray more; it's to find out why you don't have the desire to pray."[1]

Full stop.

I couldn't believe my professor had said those words out loud. I thought I was the only one who often felt like prayer was another task to check off my list. His statement shook me, as it threatened to reveal my inner heart.

I've always prayed, and I imagine you have, too. I've studied prayer and have always understood its importance. Guilt shows up when I don't take time to pray. During that Spiritual Formation course, I was going through all the motions I thought would help me grow mature in my spiritual life and utilize my gifting. I'd led, taught, and written Bible studies. I even went back to school to study the Bible more thoroughly. Yet, I tried to keep a prayer journal and never kept it up. Prayer wasn't something I looked forward to doing.

I began to work through the words my professor, Dr. Coe, said. The deeper question my heart needed from the only One who held the answer rumbled around in my brain. "God, why don't I have a strong desire to pray?" I never considered saying something out loud like that, for it sounded so brutally rude (and honest). Of course I had a desire to pray. Didn't I?

Dr. Coe's months-long prayer journey intimidated me to the core. I was tasked with praying for one whole hour each week, while focused on assigned prayer topics and questions. Yet, what was even more challenging was shutting up long enough to listen to God. I recognized prayer wasn't just about talking to God; what was ahead for me was much bigger than that. I didn't know what to expect, but here's how it played out: it was awkward, frustrating, and uncomfortable.

Until it wasn't.

Hours in prayer, which had seemed endless and long, became hours that didn't last long enough. I needed more space with God because I was finally being honest with Him.

Over time, I began to see God differently. I started to give things over to Him and truly let Him lead. Trusting Him became effortless. Because of Dr. Coe's piercing questions, I finally listened.

My spiritual life was upended. I'd spent so long looking within myself and my own efforts. I'd made my relationship with God so much harder than it needed to be, so much harder than God designed it to be. This new way plunged deeper.

Not only did I pray differently, I began to live differently. I'd heard of freedom and thought I'd experienced it, yet this was bigger than I had previously known. My prayer life became enjoyable. My perspective on life changed. Sharing my faith wasn't so intimidating. God took me down a new path, and I couldn't help but notice a transformation.

Jesus discipled me as He overhauled my prayer life.

As I began to reflect on my life over the last decade, I noticed a pattern of biblical lessons God taught me and a new way of looking at prayer. Prayer no longer existed as just something I needed to do; it was the only hope for the transformation needed in my heart.

Over the next seven weeks, you, too, will be challenged to look at your relationship with Christ and prayer differently. You will take inventory of your spiritual life. You will be led into deep, raw, honest prayer with God. I'm guessing it'll be different than what you're used to in your prayer life.

Tell me if any of these resonate with you and your relationship with God:

You want to BELIEVE, so you try—hard. You say you trust God, but your heart often questions His plan.

You DECIDE to let God lead your life but refuse to let go of control in certain areas.

You SEEK His voice through His Word but don't always honor what it says.

You PRAY but aren't completely honest with God.

You desire to LIVE a life that glorifies Him, yet your human sin nature overtakes you.

You PRAISE God for all He's given you, but your attitude doesn't reflect your gratitude.

You want to SHARE your faith, but intimidation takes over.

This is not a guilt trip; it's quite the opposite. I want to rattle you, so I can tell you this: *there is so much hope*. These seven challenges describe all of us because we are all fallen sinners. If you are a believer in Christ, the power to overturn all of this is in you. But you have to access the power to experience a difference. We continuously try to live the Christian life without the Holy Spirit's influence. We attempt it in our own capacity, so we constantly fail. Then we end up burnt out, worn out, grumpy, weak, and in the grip of sin's hold. Our heart needs transformation from the only Source with the strength to change it. That's what these seven weeks are about: we are not transforming our actions; we are inviting God to transform our *nature*.

Each week you will take one step closer to God through devotional sessions and prayer. DAY ONE of each week offers a teaching. DAYS TWO through SIX present devotions that expand on the teaching. Stories or events from my own life or from characters in the Bible will help you consider what He teaches through these situations. DAY SEVEN invites you to check in with God, allowing time to make sure you're on the right track.

Prayer will be much of our focus. You will linger with at least three questions to take to God every day. I suggest writing them on an index card to take them with you. By studying His Word and seeking His heart, you will wait and watch for answers throughout your day. Then, you will have an opportunity to dive deeper into Scripture to hear Him speak further.

Allow me to prepare you for the ride: carve out time for this. I would safely say to allow five-to-six minutes for the daily reading and fifteen minutes for the dedicated prayer time. Plan it, set an alarm on your phone, turn the T.V. off, dedicate the carpool line time, hide in a closet: whatever you have to do to get the time, simply do it! Consider this a prayer boot camp, a deeper dive into your prayer life and your relationship with Christ. Be sure to give it the time it deserves because that will determine what you get out of it. Going through these seven weeks with another person or a group provides a great plan for accountability. And finally, consider getting a journal to write down the answers you receive throughout your prayer sessions.

By the end of the seven weeks, you will be equipped with seven steps to guide your prayer for any and every situation that comes into your life. That's it: seven steps over seven weeks. This is an invitation to *get over yourself*, like I had to. Let go of the self-sufficient nature that holds you captive and learn to pray like your life depends on it (*because it does*).

I am eager for you to discover what God has for you. I'm so glad you're here.

Let's dive in...

WEEK ONE

believe

DAY ONE

Choose to Believe in God's Perfect Providence

"And the Lord said to Moses, 'How long will this people despise me? And how long will they not believe in me, in spite of all the signs that I have done among them?'"

Numbers 14:11[2]

Eleven days.

That's all the time the journey from Mount Sinai to the Promised Land was supposed to last. Those eleven days manifested into forty years because of one thing: unbelief.

Yes, the Israelites disobey. Yes, they constantly complain. But God doesn't address these surface-level behaviors; He sees the heart. God knows these attitudes and actions are indicators of underlying unbelief in Him.

"...whoever believes in Him should not perish but have eternal life." John 3:16b

Belief matters. Unbelief holds tremendous power because it gives the enemy of our soul an entry point, an open door. The Israelites listen to the wrong people and doubt God's plan. Everything falls apart.

When we're disobedient to God, it's not solely because we're sinners and that's what sinners do; we're disobedient because we lack belief in God's plan. When we complain to God, it's not solely because we're human, and that's what humans do; we complain because we lack belief that what God is allowing to happen has a purpose. Our faith is weak.

Weak faith destroys lives.

One day, years ago, perhaps you stood before a group of people and professed your faith in God or experienced being baptized. Or you sat on your back porch with your parents and said a prayer accepting Jesus into your heart. Maybe you're just starting your faith journey. Whenever or however you came to faith in God, that began a lifelong, daily battle of the wills within your heart. As you've likely noticed, choosing belief in God that one time was only the beginning of this journey with God. This week we will invite God to train our hearts to choose belief in Him over unbelief in Him in every situation.

When conflicted, disobedient, or grumbling, hope is not lost because we serve a great God who delivers an abundance of grace. So, instead of wallowing in shame or guilt, we lean into a simple solution: reflection. We reflect on how God has already shown us His perfect plan in our own lives.

Why It Matters:

The Bible offers a consistent theme from Genesis to Revelation. This overarching idea—words we never actually read on the pages in reference to God—stands at the heart of the entire story: God's Divine providence.[3]

Divine providence means God guides and controls everything in the universe. He uses details, events, and circumstances for His greater good. Nothing is outside of His control. This is certainly difficult to comprehend when we look around a hurting world.

And it doesn't help that we're forgetful.

We forget all the times God came through for us. We fail to recall tiny details He used to bring us to where we are today. We disregard all the good He's made out of such evil around us. We overlook how much He's protected us from, things we are unable to picture.

Here's something we need not forget: we live in a fallen world. Much happens we simply can't grasp. Hear this truth: we can fixate on evil, or we can fixate on Him. We have that choice.

What It Takes:

This week's step is to choose to believe in God's perfect providence. You'll take an honest look at your life, where you are now, and what God has walked through with you.

Allow Him to remind you of all the times you've trusted Him as well as times you didn't trust Him and took matters into your own hands. Through Scriptures, lessons, and prayer, let this be the week you step forward into the next set of circumstances that come your way and choose to trust He is working it all together for your good and His glory. Learn to grow and rest in His perfect providence.

How to Get There:

I cannot change your heart, and neither can you. The One who holds your heart is the One with the power to transform it into everything He created it to be and everything you desire to be in Him. Take inventory of your spiritual life today. Do it with Him.

Prayer Points

1. Lord, in what ways have You used the darkest points in my life for good in my life?

2. How have You shown me that I can trust you in both the good and the bad?

3. What behavior is masking unbelief in my life?

4. What purpose have You shown me in all You've allowed me to go through?

Allow time with these powerful questions. Take a breath. Let God lead your memories and thoughts where He wants them to go.

Dig Deeper

Meditate on this Scripture by reading then praying it. Allow the Holy Spirit to write it on your heart and reveal something new to you. This verse will be referenced this week and in the coming weeks:

"But he said to me, 'My grace is sufficient for you, for my power is made perfect in weakness.' Therefore I will boast all the more gladly of my weaknesses, so that the power of Christ may rest upon me. For the sake of Christ, then, I am content with weaknesses, insults, hardships, persecutions, and calamities. For when I am weak, then I am strong." 2 Corin. 12:9-10

WEEK ONE

believe

DAY TWO

God's Ever Steady Presence

"But he said to me, 'My grace is sufficient for you, for my power is made perfect in weakness.' Therefore I will boast all the more gladly of my weaknesses, so that the power of Christ may rest upon me. For the sake of Christ, then, I am content with weaknesses, insults, hardships, persecutions, and calamities. For when I am weak, then I am strong." 2 Corin. 12:9-10

I typically experience my most enjoyable times in prayer when I'm walking. I said typically. It can turn out one of two ways: the first way feels like a happy dance. I can't wait to have dedicated time with God. I smile at the birds singing to me while I talk to Him. I head back home excited to dive into Scripture. God confirms things throughout the day. We are beautifully in sync.

The second kind of walk tempts me to blare music or fire up a podcast. I'm convinced the birds aim to attack me. My enthusiasm for talking with God sizzles. I go home feeling obligated to read the Bible. I feel I "should." Prayer exists on a surface level as it's just another chore on the checklist.

Have you felt this teeter-totter in your relationship with God? Theology names these seasons: spiritual consolation and spiritual desolation. Let's look at what these words mean.

Spiritual Consolation: Overall, you *feel* joy in being in relationship with God. He reinforces your behavior with feeling His presence and spiritual joy. He allows the gift of experiencing His close presence.

Spiritual Desolation: During these times, God doesn't feel close. You pray, serve, and read the Bible. Detached and feeling far-off, there's no payoff. No answers appear when you pray. You feel lonely. God feels distant.

Why it Matters:

We're tempted to feel as though times of spiritual desolation are punishment for not trying hard enough to maintain His presence.

As if we're in control.

Instead, what if God desires to reveal something in times of desolation?

God may be withdrawing spiritual pleasure, yet He is not withdrawing Himself. Read that again. He is still very present and very much at work. However, the Spirit is at work in our heart. We are in the process of learning to love Him by faith alone, regardless of feelings.

He's asking you: "Are you only in this relationship for the feeling, the payoff? Are you chasing a spiritual experience?"

"Or do you love Me because you love Me?"

God is never distant. He simply trusts us enough to move us forward in our maturity, as if He's telling us we're ready.

It's no different than parental expectations. As children progress in their maturity, parents' expectations increase. The same is true of our heavenly Father. By removing the pleasure of feeling close, we become hungry for Him. We begin to seek Him in new ways. We open our heart to what He reveals. He exposes the truth of what is in our heart, places we have filled up with ourselves as the focus, rather than being filled up with the Spirit. Ultimately, He shows our need for absolute dependence on Him. As Paul says, "for the sake of Christ, then, I am content with weaknesses, insults, hardships, persecutions, and calamities. For when I am weak, then I am strong." (2Corin. 12:10). Then, *His* power is on display.

What it Takes:

What if we viewed these times of desolation as a gift? And then, what if we respond the same way as we do in those times of consolation when He does feel present and we're getting all the reward? We still draw near to Him just as passionately with a surrendered posture. We are open to what He's doing.

We pray and read His Word to access whatever feeling He wants to give us because it's His to give and ours to accept. Here, we recognize that it's certainly not ours to control or manufacture. We simply access grace that's been given to us by bringing Him our heart.

How to Get There:

Let's take the spiritual growth out of our own hands and put it in the hands of the One who can do something with it.

Prayer Points

1. God, how are You drawing me closer to You in the midst of the season I'm in now?

2. In what ways am I accessing the grace You've given me? In what ways am I going through the motions?

3. How do I tend to react in these different seasons? How am I not trusting You?

Dig Deeper

Read Paul's words in 2 Corinthians 12. Consider what season you are in. Reflect on when you were in the opposite season. What can you add to your daily routine to keep your focus on Him having your whole heart?

WEEK ONE

believe

DAY THREE

Covenant for the Win

"For if you keep silent at this time, relief and deliverance will rise for the Jews from another place, but you and your father's house will perish. And who knows whether you have not come to the kingdom for such a time as this?" Esther 4:14

I might have run away.

Living in ancient Persia, married to the king whose favorite pastime included killing people, knowing my head might be next on the docket if I made one wrong move, I might have run away. As much as being a queen sounds great in theory, I might have run far, far away. Or at least kept my mouth shut.

But not this woman.

I could use a dose of her bravery.

Meet Esther, queen of ancient Persia. Her older cousin Mordecai speaks to her in this text. He's important in this story, too, as he stepped in and adopted Esther when her parents died. More of a father or uncle figure, Mordecai possesses wisdom, loves God, and loves her.

Esther becomes queen in a rather whirlwind, unromantic, horrendous kind of way. (Esther 1-3). Smitten with Esther, the king loves power, thrives on it, and will do anything he can to keep his power or gain even more power.

Enter Haman. This guy hates Mordecai, and he hates Jews. He talks the king into killing all the Jews in all 127 provinces because they threaten the king's power. Oh, and by the way, Mordecai and Esther are both Jews, yet no one knows that fact.

Now, the last part of this verse historically garners bumper sticker attention. Yet what strikes me is what Mordecai says right before his famous line, "for such a time as this." See, it doesn't quite make the necessary impact unless the previous sentence is appreciated. In that previous line, Esther is inspired by Mordecai's faith. He displayed it so beautifully through this statement: "...relief and deliverance will rise for the Jews from another place." Considering all that is going on, it's an interesting thing to say.

An edict declares that all the Jews are to be killed on a certain day in the next eleven months. Mordecai tells Esther this fact and then asks her to talk to the king. Admittedly, she's not the kind of queen who has dinner with the king daily. He entertains plenty of other ladies who keep him warm at night, so Esther hasn't even seen him in thirty days. If she goes to the king unannounced, she risks losing her life. Her husband, who doesn't know she's Jewish, is unpredictable. He banished the last queen who ticked him off.

Why it Matters:

If Esther chooses to approach the king, she will have to put everything on the line, including her very life. She has a choice. Mordecai knows this. Yet he knows something else: God made a covenant with the Jews years earlier. The Jews are His chosen people whom He promised to protect. If Mordecai is going to challenge Esther to live out her faith in God, then they both have to believe God will hold up His end of the bargain.

God always does.

What it Takes:

He will save His people with Esther or without her. So, she faces a choice: be a part of God's plan or don't be a part of God's plan. Putting her life on the line isn't just a risk, it's an immense opportunity. Be a part of saving God's people and be used by God in a mighty way.

Or don't.

Jesus' death on the cross fulfilled a New Covenant between God and us (Jer. 31:31-34), so we face the same choice as Esther: be part of God's plan or don't be part of God's plan.

Do you, like me, need a dose of Esther's bravery?

How to Get There:

Consider what God is inviting you to in this season of life. What would it take for you to leap forward into obedience with such bravery?

In God's perfect providence, He will achieve what He needs to, with or without us. We just miss out when we don't participate.

Prayer Points

1. God, what might You be calling me to in light of where You have placed me?

2. How can I glorify you in this situation?

3. What fears hold me back from being obedient?

Dig Deeper

Read Esther 4 in its entirety. Watch Esther make the scariest decision of her life and see how God shows up.

WEEK ONE

believe

DAY FOUR

Those Unresolved Relationships

"Accordingly, though I am bold enough in Christ to command you to do what is required, yet for love's sake I prefer to appeal to you—I, Paul, an old man and now a prisoner also for Christ Jesus—I appeal to you for my child, Onesimus, whose father I became in my imprisonment. (Formerly he was useless to you, but now he is indeed useful to you and to me.)" Philemon 8-11

Hands down, if I could have anyone over for dinner, alive or dead, it would be the apostle Paul. He only solidified his spot for that place recently after I studied his letter to Philemon. It opened up to me a whole other realm of what he was like in real life. The man's personality had some levels of complexity! Watch as we see how he masterfully deals with people in a God-honoring, yet firm manner.

Not only does he respectively pull off passive-aggressive language, but he demonstrates how to restore a broken relationship in just twenty-five verses. By the end, we get a picture of God's design for forgiveness, restitution, and reconciliation.

He greets Philemon at the beginning of the letter as a "prisoner of Christ," not as an "apostle of Christ," as he does in most of his other letters. Perhaps this signifies their close relationship. Notice he says, not a prisoner of Rome, a prisoner of Christ. Love that.

After spending a few sentences buttering Philemon up, Paul appeals to him about his runaway slave Onesimus. Now, we're all familiar with slavery being motivated by race in the last few hundred years, but that just wasn't the case in the Roman Empire, where approximately 25% of the population were slaves. That's 16 million people. Often, slaves were acquired through warfare, as orphaned children, or people sold themselves or their children into slave labor to pay off their debt. Slaves had no rights and were considered property until they could pay off their debt. Many slaves served regular jobs like being managers or doctors.

Here's the story. Onesimus (pronounced O-ness-i-mus) was Philemon's slave, whom he had bought. This meant that if Onesimus ran off, he owed a debt because his life had monetary value. So, if he runs away, he was considered a thief because *he* was Philemon's property. Onesimus runs off anyway.

He providentially meets Paul 1,000 miles away. Paul leads him to the Lord. The two connect as brothers in service to God. Paul sees God's transformation of Onesimus' life and wants him to be forgiven and restored to Philemon.

Paul also led Philemon to Christ years earlier, so he draws upon this authority in this letter, but does so humbly... kind of. This is where another glimpse of Paul shows up.

He says, "though I am bold enough in Christ to command you to do what is required, yet for love's sake, I prefer to appeal to you." (verse 8b). Essentially, he could utilize this spiritual father/mentor role, but he's not going to do so. Instead, Paul offers a gentle reminder of all he has done for Philemon. And then reminds Philemon of Paul's age (an old man) and his current status (a prisoner), just in case Philemon forgot. Slick.

Why it Matters:

Paul is saying that he's sending Onesimus back to Philemon. Paul volunteers to take on Onesimus' debt. He asks Philemon to see Onesimus in a new light and to be reconciled with him.

What it Takes:

Paul is asking Philemon to forgive Onesimus. He's personally taken care of the restitution. He implies an apology is coming. He describes a change of heart in the man. Only then is he asking for reconciliation.

Paul paid the debt for Onesimus just like Jesus did for us. Onesimus received grace he didn't deserve, the same grace dealt to us daily. Isn't this an incredible biblical formula for reconciliation in relationships in a way that honors God?

How to Get There:

God is always at work behind the scenes. I don't know if you have relationships that need work, but I sure do. Read through this story. Let yourself get to know Paul a little better. Take these lessons straight to God in prayer today.

Prayer Points

1. God, I have people I struggle to forgive. What is causing me to struggle so hard to do so?

2. I also have people I grapple to reconcile with, God. How do I determine if it's necessary? Show me when it's appropriate and when it's not in each relationship.

3. How are You working in this relationship? How can I better surrender it to You and trust You to use it for Your glory?

Dig Deeper

Go read Philemon. Specifically, reflect on verse 18. Who has already done that for you? Take that thought with you today.

WEEK ONE

believe

DAY FIVE

When It Hurts

"Then the Lord said to Jacob, 'Return to the land of your fathers and to your kindred, and I will be with you.'" Gen. 31:3

I feel manipulated.

This is the puddle I've sat in for the past year. Someone I trusted had an agenda. I was part of it. Now it's imploding. I thought God was doing something great through me since I was being obedient. I hate knowing I've been part of something I don't ultimately agree with.

Even though I got out of the situation, I'm forced to do nothing and wait to see what God does with the mess.

I have no control over any of it.

Why it Matters:

Prior to the scene in Genesis 31, we watch Laban manipulate Jacob repeatedly (Gen. 29:14-30, 30:25-43). Jacob was strung along and now he's sick of Laban's tactics yet doesn't want a confrontation.

I can relate to Jacob.

Even though he's scared, annoyed, and tired of the antics, he doesn't flee immediately. Instead, Jacob waits until God tells him to go (Gen 31:3). See, he was paying attention. He saw what God was doing and acted in obedience.

Jacob's backstory wasn't perfect (Gen. 27:5-46). He was a sinner and not always virtuously motivated; a broken person whose heart God was still at work on. Regardless of his past or his feelings, Jacob saw God working and trusted Him.

God brought restoration to this family. It came in the form of a covenant between Jacob and Laban (v. 44), in the form of a pillar (v. 45) and a heap (v. 46) to serve as a witness and a boundary—they agreed to do no harm to each other (v. 52). Only God!

What it Takes:

What does this text tell us to do when we find ourselves like Jacob?

1. Pause. Don't react when emotions are high.

2. Look for God at work and trust Him.

3. Act in obedience.

This is not a time to pray for justice or vindication. Instead, watch for what God reveals about Himself, what He asks you to do next, and who He needs you to be through the situation.

Manipulation is a result of the fall. If we filter Jacob's situation through the truth of God's Word, then we know He created Jacob and Laban in His image to fulfill the purpose He had for each of them. God knew they would sin and would need redemption. Jesus' eventual death on the cross would cover it and bring ultimate restoration.

God is not done working on any of us in the hurting place we're in, no matter how broken we are. So, there's no sense in losing hope. We, too, have Jesus' promises of full restoration, whether in this life or the next.

During my own struggles, I now see God's perfect providence opening up doors. I see where He's been working on healing my heart and preparing and pruning me for what's next. It wasn't until I paused that I could see what Jacob saw.

How to Get There:

Jacob waited on God, let Him lead, and stepped out in obedience. God was sovereign over Jacob's story and is sovereign over my story.

He's sovereign over yours, too. Will you trust Him with what you're facing?

Prayer Points

1. God, how can I better control my actions when others hurt or manipulate me?

2. What is it You need me to do in the situation I'm facing now? Fight or let you fight?

3. How can I keep my focus on You and let go of trying to control?

4. What are You revealing to me about You?

Dig Deeper

Read Genesis 31. Watch Jacob's actions and reactions.

WEEK ONE

believe

DAY SIX

After the Funeral

"Though you have made me see troubles, many and bitter, you will restore my life again; from the depths of the earth you will again bring me up. You will increase my honor and comfort me once more." Psalm 71:20-21 NIV

Two weeks had passed. Two long, gut-wrenching weeks. Two harrowing weeks that seemed to move in slow motion. Sneaking away to steal a break from my baby's and toddler's demands, I stood at my kitchen counter, staring at the card in my hand.

Unbeknownst to me, it would be the last of the sympathy cards, yet it would have a bigger impact than I could have imagined. I received the card from a dear friend, one who showed up the week he died. She showed up just to watch my children so I could take a long hot shower and sink deep into my first good cry. Lord knows, my friend, she's one of the good ones.

My brother served in the Army. When he returned home from his second tour, he just wasn't the same. The light had vanished from his eyes. Between his fierce battle with PTSD and a traumatic brain injury, addiction came. We prayed. We staged an intervention. We tried all we knew to try.

The funeral was brutal. Those first few days slipped by in a blur as we were just trying to get through the days. I moved about in terrible pain; one minute heartbroken, the next I was mad, then I was numb. I felt everything. I felt nothing. Afterwards, life seemed to go on for everyone else, but I wasn't okay. I was still mourning and yet didn't know how to grieve.

Then I got the card from my dear friend.

Inside, she included the Scripture that would change everything for me:

"Though you have made me see troubles, many and bitter,

you will restore my life again;

from the depths of the earth

you will again bring me up.

You will increase my honor

and comfort me once more."

Psalm 71:20-21

I plopped down into my kitchen chair and sobbed. I pictured my brother running into the arms of Jesus. I saw a smile on his face that I hadn't seen in years. For days, I unintentionally meditated on this verse. I trusted the Holy Spirit would reveal what He needed to as I let God into a place of my heart He wanted to mend. I let this verse teach me who God is in His perfect love and mercy, and what His promises say.

Why it Matters:

My brother's death did not escape God's perfect providence because he now experiences what lies ahead for me one day. See, God didn't choose to restore my brother in this earthly life; He brought him Home to do that. In heaven, his honor is completely restored. My brother is perfect, happy, and comforted. Now I see. God began to heal my heart that day. I moved into a season of accepting his death. In the years since, God has shifted me forward in the direction of pointing others to Him in the midst of their own pain.

Meditation on that verse led to accidental memorization. God wrote it on my heart years ago because I needed it then to trust His plan. Now, when I start to feel grief creep into those places God has already healed, I can cling to this verse. I remind myself of the truth God showed me: He used the worst thing that ever happened in my life for His glory. So, when I see a guy that looks like my brother in a crowd and my heart drops into my stomach, or I tell a story about his shenanigans and laugh until I cry, or I see his spitting image in his kids and I slip into grieving him all over again, the Holy Spirit prompts my heart with this verse.

What it Takes:

Instead of giving the enemy a foothold on my grief, I give the Holy Spirit a foothold on my healing. That is the power of clinging to and memorizing Scripture. The Holy Spirit draws upon it constantly to work stuff out in me.

How to Get There:

I challenge you to do the same: memorize Scripture. Cling to it, and ask the Holy Spirit to use it. God certainly restored my brother, but He restored me too. There is a future beyond today's grief. Invite Him into the pain and watch as He heals and then utilizes it for your good and His glory.

Prayer Points

1. Lord, what am I still grieving?

2. What Scriptures would speak life to me that I could commit to memory?

3. How can I better trust in Your perfect providence, even in the midst of grief?

Dig Deeper

Read Psalm 71. Picture David pouring out his heart to God in the midst of trouble and exhaustion. Highlight verses 20-21 in your Bible as a reminder of the promise we have of heaven.

WEEK ONE

believe

DAY SEVEN

Check-In Day

How am I choosing to believe in God's perfect providence?

Today offers an opportunity for you to take a breath. Take time to determine in conversation with God whether you are leaning into the transformation He has in store for you. Choosing to believe and trust in God's perfect providence isn't solely about focusing on *what* God gives to us. Sometimes, it's trusting the *when* or the *how*.

Remember: God gives grace, a lot of it. If this has been a tough week and you haven't given prayer the time you wanted to, *guilt is not the answer*. Honest prayer is. If this has been an incredible week and you can't believe all He has shown you, take time to pray and tell Him thank you. Either way, go for a walk outside, around your basement, or on a treadmill. Move your body as you pray. Something about the motion allows the mind to work better. Just a theory but try it!

This isn't a time for you to check in with me or with yourself; it's a check in with God. How have you chosen to take Step One: Choosing to *believe* in God's Perfect Providence?

Prayer Points

Take extra time in prayer. Choose the questions that apply to you:

1. Lord, this week has been incredible in prayer with You. I am grateful that You have shown me _____.

2. Father, distractions won this week, but Your grace wins every time. How can I better prioritize my time to allow this relationship with You to thrive? What is going on in my heart that I haven't made this time with You of the most importance?

3. God, this week, You have shown me all the ways I can and should trust in Your perfect providence. This is my heart's desire. What areas of doubt still linger in me?

4. Lord, I am deciding to trust in Your perfect providence in every situation. How will You remind me and convict me

of this every time I start to doubt? How can I hold myself accountable?

Memorize

Write down these seven steps. Begin to memorize them:

BELIEVE

DECIDE

SEEK

PRAY

LIVE

PRAISE

SHARE

WEEK TWO

decide

DAY ONE

Decide to Let God Lead

"But I say, walk by the Spirit, and you will not gratify the desires of the flesh. For the desires of the flesh are against the Spirit, and the desires of the Spirit are against the flesh, for these are opposed to each other, to keep you from doing the things you want to do. But if you are led by the Spirit, you are not under the law." Galatians 5:16-18

My life reflects the choices I've made. I chose to be dumb and faced the consequences. Others chose to be selfish, and I felt the effects. It's said that the average adult makes up to 35,000 choices a day. Our lives can take that many different directions based on those choices.

Why It Matters:

I believe that God chose us. He made the first move in the relationship (John 6:44), and we responded. However, this chapter will not be a conversation about Reformed theology, election, or free will. (There is a wonderful resource I will recommend at the end of this week.) Instead, we will focus on what we *do* have control over: the daily decisions we make that bring us closer to Christ or farther away. How are we setting ourselves up to let God lead our life?

You've likely grown up in the Christian faith or been walking with Christ for a while. For as long as I can remember, I have walked with Christ. Maybe, like me, you've noticed that the ups and downs in your relationship with Him reflect the choices you've made.

Last week centered on choosing to believe in God's perfect providence in every circumstance. I hope you took the time to work this out in your own heart with God. There's no greater foundation in our faith than starting there with Him.

Today, we will ask Him to prepare our hearts to let Him lead our life.

God is constantly forming our spirit (Romans 12:1-2) and desires continuous transformation in us. His plans are good, *so good*, but we get in the way. We refuse to release control to Him. We determine, instead, we would do a better job forming our own spirit—even as Christians.

Let's do a case study...

Picture this person with me: we'll call her Emma Sue.

Emma Sue is a woman who is sweet-as-pie. Works hard, pays her taxes. Raises kind, respectful children. A great friend; would give you the shirt off her back. Emma would never cheat on her husband. She's loyal, honest, and kind. In my mind, she must be Southern. She would be considered moral, a woman of virtue.

Do you assume she's a Christian?

See, Emma Sue doesn't feel she needs God. She is perfectly content with being a good, moral person in her own power. Because when she does this well, she gets the glory.

The apostle Paul would refer to this spiritual formation as "in the flesh," a term he used over 90 times in the New Testament. As John Piper explains, "Flesh is any human action or achievement without dependence upon the Holy Spirit and without glorifying, exalting in, trusting, treasuring, and valuing Jesus Christ."[4] So, he's talking about moralism and virtue—all seemingly good things—but, in Emma Sue's case, these things sit under her own control and power.

Theology names three different categories for attempting to form our spirit by ourselves[5]:

- Secular spiritual formation

- Religion

- "New Age Mystical" spiritual formation

The first one—"secular spiritual formation"—means to do things according to the world's way, with the world's standards of right and wrong.

A second way is by "religion": following a set of rules and recognizing that your task is to obey said rules to earn salvation or favor from God, or whatever Being is receiving the worship. When one does this well and obeys the rules, the person becomes prideful and arrogant. But when they don't succeed, great shame and guilt exist within the person. Paul would once again call this living "in the flesh," still in one's own power.

Pride, arrogance, shame, guilt. Any of these resonate?

The last way is "New Age Mystical" spiritual formation. This is when someone believes in some type of Divinity, but it's more aligned with "awakening yourself to the god within." One's spirit is formed by a "spiritual awakening," a "self-actualization," or the "Law of Attraction." Many self-help books are geared toward this last way of thinking. Paul addresses this specifically in Colossians, as the church was battling this type of influence heavily.

All of these ways are against God's design. But we can certainly choose them, even as Christians.

What it Takes:

In the Christian life, God-centered Spiritual Formation involves the work of the Holy Spirit. Instead of the work we're so used to weighing ourselves down with, it involves the challenging task of surrender. Total surrender to God is not a single, one-time decision. It consists of repeated everyday choices made in every aspect of our life and every aspect of our heart.

As Christians, do we always walk in the Spirit?

No, we don't, but we're surely capable of it. We have access and opportunity. We see in 2 Peter 1:3-4 that we have been given all we need to live a godly life. However, we must utilize what's available. We are capable of walking "in the flesh," like those who don't know Christ. We are still susceptible to allow outside influences to form our spirit.

Even when we are doing things we believe to be "good," we still have the capability and the temptation of doing "good" in our own power. We are trying to do God's work for Him for the sake of our own glory. I think this one stings the worst for me.

God does want us to live moral lives, but He wants us to do it through Him, in His power. He knows something we may not want to admit: we are going to fail if we go forward in our own power. He is perfect in every attribute He possesses, and I don't think I need to reiterate that we simply *aren't perfect.*

How to Get There:

When we allow Him to produce Christlikeness through us, it works out for our good, and He gets the glory (Romans 8:28). By abiding in Him and maintaining open communication, He does the work.

This week may be more difficult. I'm asking you to consider questions and Scriptures. Then, take them to God in raw, honest prayer.

Prayer Points

1. Father, in what areas am I trying to be good in my own capacity?

2. Lord, am I struggling or growing weary because I'm not producing the results in life that *I* want?

3. Where do I harbor pride, arrogance, shame, or guilt in my heart because I've tried to follow a religion instead of You?

4. In what ways am I allowing something other than the Holy Spirit to form my spirit?

5. How am I letting You lead my life? What am I refusing to surrender?

Dig Deeper

In light of today's reading, read Galatians 5:16-18 again. Then, reflect on these words:

"We've been called to have dominion over the earth to the glory of God, but we want dominion for the 'glory' of man...Nothing built for the glory of man will survive His scrutiny. But what is done for God's glory will endure forever." R.C. Sproul[6]

- How do we know that we are doing anything for God's glory? "Nothing built for the glory of man" is a good starting prayer point for this: "God, am I building my life for my glory or Yours?"

WEEK TWO

decide

DAY TWO

Why doesn't God make it easier on us?

"Abide in me, and I in you. As the branch cannot bear fruit by itself, unless it abides in the vine, neither can you, unless you abide in me."
John 15:4

I love my son, but man, my kid is the worst person to watch movies with because the questions never stop!

"What's that guy doing? Why is he doing that?"

"Where are they going? Why are they doing that?"

My answer is the same every time he asks, "I have just as much information as you!"

Since I'm his mom, he assumes I have all the answers. My job his whole life has been to lead him, teach him, and answer all of his "why" questions. Of course, I want to continue to be that person, but as he grows and matures in knowledge, my role changes.

Why it Matters:

Sometimes, when I pray, I feel like my son, asking perpetual questions. I wonder if God gets impatient with me!

I heard of a conversation between two Christian theologian professors. They discussed why New Testament authors don't give more specific instructions about how to ward off sin. Couldn't God have given a four-step approach to rid us of anger, jealousy, pride, and the rest of the daily issues we face? Wouldn't that reduce the sin in the world and bring us closer to Christ? We'd have a lot fewer questions for God!

The older professor wisely shared three beautifully profound yet simple reasons. He explained that God did not prompt those authors with such specific directions because:

1. It forces us to depend on Him vs. being dependent on a how-to system (Romans 5). Following a four-step how-to system or a set of rules is transactional. It takes the power into our own hands and moves us away from the One who can produce a lasting heart change. If we want deep character change, we must follow God's design. As my professor

Dr. Coe said, "I don't just want God to take away my anger. I want to become a person who is not easily angered."

- ○ God calls us to abide in Him. If we spend our entire lives simply following a set of rules, then we have no reason to have a relationship with Him. God went to great lengths to allow us to call on Him. This is the difference between a *religion* and a *relationship.*

2. <u>We become open to our own development, gain wisdom, and grow in our faith.</u> James tells us trials are opportunities. God uses everything!

- ○ "Count it all joy, my brothers, when you meet trials of various kinds, for you know that the testing of your faith produces steadfastness. And let steadfastness have its full effect, that you may be perfect and complete, lacking in nothing. If any of you lacks wisdom, let him ask God, who gives generously to all without reproach, and it will be given to him." James 1:2-5

3. <u>We come to understand that God wants us to do it together within community, to learn from each other, and share.</u>

- ○ Hebrews 10:24-25 says, "And let us consider how to stir up one another to love and good works, not neglecting to meet together, as is the habit of some, but encouraging one another, and all the more as you see the Day drawing near."

What it Takes:

God's design is for us to rely on Him, mature in our growth, and be in community with other believers. What if we embraced this design instead of fighting it?

How to Get There:

Our Heavenly Father loves His children's questions, as He tells us to ask, seek, and knock (Matt 7:7-8). Commit today to continue asking questions that set you on the path He has prepared for you, questions that position you to be open to what He has for you. He's listening.

We have one very patient heavenly Father.

Prayer Points

1. God, how can I move from transactional prayers to relational prayers?

2. In what ways am I not maturing in the community of believers You have blessed me with?

3. What areas of my life am I not truly abiding in You?

Dig Deeper

Out of the three areas listed in "Why It Matters," which one do you struggle with the most? Write down a verse or two of the Scripture connected with it. Ponder it today.

WEEK TWO

decide

DAY THREE

What Does Your Life Point Toward?

"He was not the light, but came to bear witness about the light."
John 1:8

"Not everything is a spiritual issue." This comment from a friend 13 years ago still resurfaces in my brain now and then. I can't say I disagree entirely, but a part of me does because I've noticed that God uses things I wouldn't expect to achieve what He needs to. If we look at His Word, He's been doing it since the beginning of time.

Why it Matters:
Each story of the Bible reveals an aspect of the Christian life from

which we can learn a lesson and apply it to our daily Christian walk. Typically, we feel we are to emulate the *character* of those we read about in each story, but what if they serve a grander purpose?

These individuals were all humans, all sinners. Though we can learn from their triumphs and failures, it seems the stronger call is to be more like them in their *focus*, as each was flawed in their character. If we look back at the people within His Word, these men and women of God aren't pointing us to themselves in their everyday lives; they're pointing us to Him.

Abraham's story ultimately points to the coming Messiah, promised to be from his bloodline. David, more of the same. Moses brought us the Law: God's expectations of living a life that honors and focuses on Him. Nehemiah knew what was at stake in protecting God's people, and his story points to the coming Savior. Esther's focus was on saving God's people, and the entire book showcases God's providence: protecting, saving, and preserving His people. Esther knew the importance of the bloodline of God's chosen people—the promise of the Savior to come. The apostle John lays it out for us in today's verse describing John the Baptist's focus, "He was not the light, but came to bear witness about the light". His life pointed to Christ.

Then Jesus is born. Now, it's all about seeing and believing He's actually here. All that's been hoped and prayed for has come true. The Messiah has arrived, just as God promised.

It's all about Him.

Jesus teaches His disciples, disciples who walk away from their entire lives to follow Him. It was an enormous choice they had the privilege to make. And they did.

Because it's all about Him.

He dies—a horrible, gruesome death for all of us—but he rises. Then, the church is born, and it becomes all about the Great Commission: go tell the world about Him. And they do. Then Paul does! And the world begins to hear the news about Christ.

Because it's *still* all about Him.

See, nothing has changed. From the beginning of time to Paul's letters, to John telling us everything to come when Jesus returns, the central focus remains: one Person, one goal, one focus.

What It Takes:
Maybe not everything in our lives is a spiritual issue, but how could we reposition our lives to bring God glory?

How To Get There:
How could your life today could point to and focus on Him? Pay attention to opportunities He gives you and reposition as needed.

Prayer Points

1. God, in what ways does my lifestyle point to you?

2. How am I displaying my trust in You to others?

3. Am I representing You well in my interactions with non-Christians and Christians alike?

Dig Deeper
Read Ephesians 4. Consider these words as you go about your day.

WEEK TWO

decide

DAY FOUR

How?

"For by him all things were created, in heaven and on earth, visible and invisible, whether thrones or dominions or rulers or authorities—all things were created through him and for him. And he is before all things, and in him all things hold together." Colossians 1:16-17

How can you glorify God right where you've been placed?

The decorations are set, and the weather is perfect. The other aunts and I greet the bride and the bridal shower guests. We invite them to sit down for a festive dinner. Before the dinner, as I prepared a devotion, I reflected on the wedding day ahead, celebrating the upcoming marriage of two young people I adore. I kept going back to the beginning—the beginning of their relationship and then the beginning of time.

Let me share a little about these two: their faith has been a huge part of the equation since the start of their relationship. It has also been a considerable part of their conversations with each other. See, they never pretended to have all the answers. They spoke with honesty about their faith and sought the Lord together. They've been doing all the right things: reading together, discussing doubts, and seeking God's will over their life. As much as I wanted this bridal shower to be all sunshine and butterflies, I also wanted to ensure they came away with something deeper to take into marriage.

You can prepare for marriage by reading all the books then marry the most fantastic human you've ever met, yet life will still happen. Things occur beyond your control. There will be things *in* your control that you mess up! There's something, however, that we can't lose sight of, so let's go back to the beginning of time:

"For by him all things were created, in heaven and on earth, visible and invisible, whether thrones or dominions or rulers or authorities—all things were created through him and for him. And he is before all things, and in him all things hold together." Colossians 1:16-17

Why it Matters:

We were created for God; He was not created for us. So, regarding this topic, what was marriage created for?

We often think of all the ideologies associated with marriage, such as love, so essential and certainly biblical! Then there's serving, respecting, submitting, and forgiving—all part of God's design for a healthy, God-honoring marriage. However, those are secondary to the sole purpose of marriage—and that is to glorify God. Loving, serving, submitting, respecting—that's how we do it. But the focus and the goal is to glorify God in this relationship. That's how we "keep God at the center."

This is easy to lose sight of in tough situations. We tend to ask God all kinds of questions like "Why? Why is this happening? Why did you allow this, God?"

What it Takes:

We are called to ask a different question.

I read singer/songwriter Laura Story's book recently. It described her life and some of the huge challenges she and her husband have faced. As she described the struggles they faced, Laura did something beautiful. She proposed a very important question to replace the typical question of "Why?"

She said, "Man asks 'Why?' Jesus asks, 'How?' Man asks, 'Why did this happen?" Jesus asks, 'How might my Father's glory be displayed through this situation?'"[7]

How to Get There:

How? How can I glorify God? That's it. Our secret to life. And it's certainly not limited to marriage.

How can I glorify God today at work? How can I glorify God today in this conflict I have? Take this with you today. When you're tempted to ask God why He is allowing something to happen or why you are so disappointed, instead, ask God, "How can Your glory be displayed in this situation?"

Prayer Points

1. How might my Father's glory be displayed through this situation?

2. How can I honor you with this next decision?

3. How can I glorify You in this relationship?

Dig Deeper

Read Colossians 1. Note how the people of Colossae and Paul both chose to glorify God right where they were placed.

WEEK TWO

decide

DAY FIVE

Kingdom Focus

"Jesus answered, 'My kingdom is not of this world. If my kingdom were of this world, my servants would have been fighting, that I might not be delivered over to the Jews. But my kingdom is not from the world.'" John 18:36

The Jewish leaders' desperation was palpable. They have had enough of Jesus' message and are ready for Him to be brought down. They know they can't kill Him under their own law, so they scheme and plot for the government to kill the Man who ultimately came to save them.

All rules, no guts. And absolutely no faith.

Weren't they paying attention to the Word they so closely upheld? The Messiah is here, and they can't accept it.

And what does Jesus do? Complies. Goodness gracious, I read this and want Him to fight the way I would and let them know the error of their thinking! Instead, Jesus does what Jesus does: shares the truth of the Gospel with Pilate. He tells Pilate the important eternal stuff, not what would keep Him off the cross. While this message goes over Pilate's head and misses his heart, it's here for us 2,000 years later: Keep the Kingdom focus.

Why it Matters:

What speaks to me the most in this scene is the lesson Jesus screams through His silence. Amid the lies and the pain He knows will come, He stays silent and withstands everything. Yes, He did that for you and me, but ultimately, He's presenting the perfect example of how we should live.

What it Takes:

Jesus lives out a prayer that answers what we long for in every relationship, every unforeseen circumstance, and every bit of suffering we face. It is right here before us as we see the perfect example from our Savior. The prayer of His heart that day was one He didn't have to ask, but you and I do. "Father, show me how to bring You glory right where I've been placed."

Jesus knew what He had to do and why. I don't know about you, but it's not always clear to me. Fortunately, Jesus didn't come into this situation empty-hearted. Directly before this scene, we find Him in a vulnerable, selfless, and specific prayer. He said, "Father, the hour has come; glorify your Son that the Son may glorify You" (John 17:1b). Jesus' desire is to bring His Father glory right where He's been placed.

How to Get There:

Jesus shows us that prayer should communicate surrendering our will and a desire to bring God glory. This exchange with Pilate is simply the aftermath of Jesus laying down His own will because He has sought the will of His Father first. He's ready. All that's left at this point is for Him to stay the course of what He came here to do: speak truth and demonstrate love. And that's precisely what He does with Pilate and His own life.

Prayer Points

1. God, how can I entirely surrender my will to You?

2. How can I honor You in the place You've put me in this season of life?

3. How can my prayers transition to be as vulnerable as Jesus' prayers were?

Dig Deeper

Read John 18 with today's perspective in mind.

WEEK TWO

decide

DAY SIX

Pause

"Therefore, I urge you, brothers and sisters, in view of God's mercy, to offer your bodies as a living sacrifice, holy and pleasing to God—this is your true and proper worship. Do not conform to the pattern of this world but be transformed by the renewing of your mind. Then you will be able to test and approve what God's will is—his good, pleasing and perfect will." Romans 12:1-2 NIV

Welcome to the "live it out" section of Romans! Paul has spent the first eleven chapters explaining faith and salvation. Now, he's essentially getting into the application part. Read the Scripture above one more time.

Why it Matters:

By the time we reach the Book of Romans, the need for dead sacrifices has been lifted. As Paul teaches here, after Jesus' final sacrifice on the cross, God now requires living sacrifices in the form of our lives. We are to offer our bodies to Him to allow Him to transform us into the person He made us to be. We are told two things: do not conform to the pattern of this world and be transformed by God. Note that Paul doesn't say, "Transform yourself." He says to "*be* transformed." By God. Just making that clear.

What it Takes:

So how does Paul tell us to live it out? Think about the last time someone close to you, your friend, neighbor, mom, husband, child, boyfriend, sister, or whoever, really exasperated you. We know we are called to love God first (Matt. 22:37). But with life's demands, it's hard to decipher how to really do that.

So, picture yourself in that moment. This person has officially acted in such a way that something in you got triggered and you went to *your crazy place*. You are about to lash out. This Scripture is showing us something very profound and practical we can do:

Step 1: **Pause.** Breathe.

Step 2: **Present.** God, I'm here.

Step 3: **Pause.** Consider who God is. Recall everything you know about Him. He is perfectly loving, perfectly merciful, and perfectly just.

Step 4: **Replace.** Ask Him to replace whatever ugly emotion emerging within you that will cause you to sin with something from His nature (love, compassion, patience, empathy).

We offer ourselves to God. We invite Him into the situation to take over. Until we get in the habit of doing this over and over, we're practicing the motions.

Two caveats are attached to this: first, it's an elementary concept. When we're at the end of ourselves with emotions flaring, we need to go back to basics. Second, when we don't lash out at people, we feel as though they will never know they need to stop their behavior. Won't we get walked all over and taken advantage of if we allow this person to treat us terribly and we choose not to react?

While that's a fair thought in theory, it doesn't consider who God is, thus skipping step three. We ask God to introduce *His* righteousness into the situation. We're saying, "I'm open and surrendered. What do You have for me?" This isn't about controlling others; it's about surrender and acknowledging the greatness of God. We're letting Him know we're not interested in wrestling Him for control.

How to Get There:

Pause - Present - Pause - Replace.

It reminds us how to prioritize our relationship with God. Here, we've invited Him in to do work on our transformation because He is the source of it.

Prayer Points

1. Lord, how have I been attempting to transform my own heart?

2. How can I incorporate these four steps of: Pause - Present - Pause - Replace into my life?

3. Where could I introduce Your righteousness into my life by simply pausing?

Dig Deeper

Reread Romans 12:1-2 slowly. Reflect on these words today.

WEEK TWO

decide

DAY SEVEN

Check-In Day

How have I decided to let God lead?

This is the question we land on today. Are you going to do it perfectly? Of course not. Have you attempted this a hundred times before? Perhaps. Allowing God to lead your life is not one more rule; it's the opportunity for freedom, a closer relationship with Him, and leads to a lot less heartache.

As you will see, at the end of these seven weeks, this will be one more step to pray through when life hits. Hold on. Stay with me; it'll all come together. This week's step focused on letting God lead. It was to help you understand what it looks like and what it takes to let Him be the One in charge. Cling to the things He's shown you. Spend extra time in prayer today as you check in with Him and see where your heart is.

Prayer Points

1. In what areas of my life do I tend to seek the glory that belongs to You?

2. Am I more comfortable "walking by the Spirit" or following a set of rules? What steps can I take to allow You to re-train my tendencies?

3. How do my daily decisions reflect a posture of surrender to Your leading?

4. What's keeping me from deciding to do it Your way? God, I desire to let you lead. I desire for you to receive the glory for the righteousness produced in my life. You're the one doing it anyway! Please help me to *decide* to allow You to lead my life in all the big and small ways.

5. Where have I truly decided to let You lead my life?

For reflection and prayer:

"But I say, walk by the Spirit, and you will not gratify the desires of the flesh. For the desires of the flesh are against the Spirit, and the desires of the Spirit are against the flesh, for these are opposed to each other, to keep you from doing the things you want to do. But if you are led by the Spirit, you are not under the law." Galatians 5:16-18

Memorize

BELIEVE

DECIDE

SEEK

PRAY

LIVE

PRAISE

SHARE

Recommended Resource (from Day 1): Norman L. Geisler, *Chosen But Free*[8]

WEEK THREE

Seek

DAY ONE

Seek His Voice by Honoring Scripture

Misinterpretation leads us away from the heart of God.

We all do it and it's totally fair that we do. We've been trained to misinterpret when told to read a passage of Scripture and see how it applies to our life. There's wisdom to this on some level, and no one here is going to discourage you from reading the Bible.

However, I want you to be diligent in considering the context.

Why it Matters:

Everything in the Bible was written in another culture, by a human (through God's prompting and leading), thousands of years ago, and with a particular purpose. Yes, it is the infallible Word of God. Yet, when we pluck it out of its original context, we can be tempted to believe that it's simply a note from God for us for this particular moment. Professor and author Walt Russell speaks accurately in his paper *Is Genre Sensitivity Really Necessary in Reading and Teaching the Bible?* He says, "It is evident in how many now assume that God speaks directly to them in the Bible. While this is true in one sense, it is not true in another. God does speak to us in the Bible, but He speaks to us through the original context of another group of people."[9]

Let's look at a familiar verse:

"For I know the plans I have for you, declares the LORD, plans to prosper you and not to harm you, plans to give you a hope and a future." Jeremiah 29:11 (NIV)

What it Takes:

This verse can change our perspective on things if we let it. However, it's part of a bigger story. The Israelites are being punished, as they had gone astray. Some even began worshiping other gods. God chooses Jeremiah to tell them they have earned some harsh discipline and will be slaves in a foreign land for 70 years, even if they are some of those that have been faithful to God. Jeremiah, a bit distraught by the thought, has a word from the Lord. He writes a letter, not to them specifically, but *to those left standing in the future.* God wants them to know it will be hard. There will be false prophets and suffering. He wants them to stay faithful and pray for their captors. He then promises the following in Jeremiah 29:10-14:

"This is what the Lord says: 'When seventy years are completed for Babylon, I will come to you and fulfill my good promise to bring you back to this place. **For I know the plans I have for you,' declares the Lord, 'plans to prosper you and not to harm you, plans to give you hope and a future.'** Then you will call on me and come and pray to me, and I will listen to you. You will seek me and find me when you seek me with all your heart. I will be found by you,' declares the Lord, 'and will bring you back from captivity. I will gather you from all the nations and places where I have banished you,' declares the Lord, 'and will bring you back to the place from which I carried you into exile.'"

Verse 11 (in bold) was for the Israelites in their specific situation: a promise to restore them after 70 years. There is much hope in this passage. God's perfect punishment and perfect plans were laid out and fulfilled. These words do not promise *us* a prosperous life here on earth. We all know we may face suffering in this life that will only be alleviated in the next life.

Someone reading or praying this Scripture without understanding its true meaning is in a dangerous mindset. They might say, "I'm not getting a prosperous life. I'm out—this whole Christianity thing is a lie."

That's not Scripture's intention.

However, what we know about this text is more about our Creator. We know He has perfect timing and cares a great deal about His children's circumstances and suffering. We can trust that He always has a plan.

When we don't consider these things, we set ourselves up to be disappointed by God, and our relationship with Him suffers. "God, you promised me a prosperous life." No, He didn't. He promised *their descendants* a prosperous life. But you know what He did promise you? Heaven. That's your hope, future, and prosperity if you have put your trust in Him.

And you know what else He promised? In Matthew 28, He says He is with you always, even until the end of the earth. He is with you. So, when we don't see the end of our suffering, the restoration of a relationship, the end of abuse, or the change of behavior we're looking for, our faith remains strong in our Redeemer because He didn't *not* do something we thought He said He *would* do. Our relationship with Him stays intact because we know God and His heart.

Misinterpretation leads us away from the heart of God.

Understanding the Scriptures in their context and interpreting them the way God intended is crucial. Being able to read Scripture on our own appropriately matures us in our faith, as Paul urges us to do in Ephesians 4 so that...

"...we will no longer be immature like children. We won't be tossed and blown about by every wind of new teaching. We will not be influenced when people try to trick us with lies so clever they sound like the truth. Instead, we will speak the truth in love, growing in every way more and more like Christ, who is the head of his body, the church." Ephesians 4:14-15 NLT

How to Get There:

When we read Scripture in context, we apply it to our lives appropriately. We honor God's Word by utilizing it the way He intended. This critical step can protect us from making Scripture about something completely irrelevant, thus dishonoring God's precious Word. Take time today to talk to God about your own method of reading Scripture and be open to what He points out to you.

Prayer Points

1. Lord, am I ever tempted to simplify Scripture too much?

2. How am I doing my due diligence to make sure I understand the context appropriately?

3. What can I do before diving into your Word to ensure I'm handling it with the honor it deserves?

Dig Deeper

If you're familiar with this Jeremiah verse, how have you interpreted it? Think through a handful of verses you know by heart. Look them up. Research, using fresh eyes. Consider:

Author/Speaker

Audience

Context

Genre

Setting

Notice how your research changes the interpretation or enhances the meaning.

WEEK THREE

Seek

DAY TWO

Who is This Guy?

"How lovely is your dwelling place, Lord Almighty! My soul yearns, even faints, for the courts of the Lord; my heart and my flesh cry out for the living God. Even the sparrow has found a home, and the swallow a nest for herself, where she may have her young—a place near your altar, Lord Almighty, my King and my God. Blessed are those who dwell in your house; they are ever praising you." Psalm 84:1-4 (NIV)

Psalm 84 invites us to worship. This expression of praise encourages our own. The author's yearning cuts straight to our hearts.

Why it Matters:

As we progress in understanding the context of God's Word, we start with the author, as this piece of information matters. When there's a piece of information missing, we cannot fully grasp or appreciate this Psalm. See, some of us get caught up reading Scripture with our mind and struggle to let it permeate our soul. Some of us sit and meditate on Scripture but miss essential details so we don't grasp what the author is getting at. Sure, it's beautiful, but there is a piece of information that is going to enable this text to explode right off the page. The thing we're missing from this Psalm when reading it without context is we don't know much about the person who is talking.

"The author (presumably a Levite who normally functioned in the temple service), now barred from access to God's house (perhaps when King Sennacherib was ravaging Judah; see 2 Kings 18:13-16), gives voice to his longing for the sweet nearness to God in his temple that he had known in the past."[10]

This is not a metaphorical door to the house of God; he's literally talking about the doorway to the Tabernacle! The most at home he has ever felt has been in the doorway of the presence of the Most High God.

And now he's without it.

This man is yearning, and you can feel it. He's talking about how fortunate a bird is who lays its nest near the altar – this guy is jealous of a bird! *Who he is* changes everything. Why?

Because he gets it.

Aside from priests, he is one of few who had been in close proximity to the presence of God. You and I cannot fathom what he saw, but we have the gift of this passage. We have his heart—his longing, his deep desiring.

What it Takes:

Consider, for a moment, the privilege we have of being a dwelling place of the Most High God. You and me, right now. Jesus' sacrifice on the cross was powerful enough to make us holy enough for God Himself to dwell in us. If that doesn't wreck your soul, consider the fact that the people of this Psalm had to embark on a pilgrimage for weeks just to be near the presence of God. How far do we have to go to experience the presence of God?

Nowhere.

If we have accepted Him as Lord of our lives, He's here—in us! Knowing what this man would have given to have what we have should elevate our appreciation for the gift of the Holy Spirit we have in us. We have the privilege of honoring His Word and utilizing this gift of the Holy Spirit.

If we had not taken a step back and recognized who the author was and where he was coming from, we would have missed all of this. We would have missed this man's heart and everything he has to tell us.

How to Get There:

Live today with deep appreciation for the gift this author showed us, the reality that we get to live out every day in the presence of the Holy Spirit.

Prayer Points

1. Lord, in what ways am I not appreciating the gift I have of the Holy Spirit in me?

2. How have I been reading Scripture solely with my mind? Solely with my heart?

3. What have I've missed in Scripture that would open up my heart and mind to something You need to say?

Dig Deeper

Go back and read Psalm 84 in its entirety through the eyes of the Doorkeeper of the house of God.

WEEK THREE

seek

DAY THREE

Influencers

"And so, from the day we heard, we have not ceased to pray for you, asking that you may be filled with the knowledge of his will in all spiritual wisdom and understanding, so as to walk in a manner worthy of the Lord, fully pleasing to him: bearing fruit in every good work and increasing in the knowledge of God; being strengthened with all power, according to his glorious might, for all endurance and patience with joy." Colossians 1:9-11

Our current culture is a lot of things: confusing, sinful, selfish, digital, loud.

I suppose not much has changed in the last 2,000 years, aside from the digital part. In the Book of Colossians, Paul addressed a group of people in Colossae who were unknowingly influenced by those in their current culture.

Why it Matters:

Since we meet the Gnostics behind the scenes of Colossians, let me explain who they were. Gnostics were New Age-type spiritual groups surrounding the new Christian church in Colossae. A specific group of Gnostics called the Essenes (pronounced uh-seenz) was especially influential. These folks strictly observed the Law of Moses but were detached from the world. The Essenes' communal way of living is like the modern cult, especially with their emphasis on the end times (often referred to as a "doomsday cult"). They believed that their knowledge was greater than any other and that the spiritual realm and the physical realm could not co-exist. Jesus being both God and Man was heretical (blatantly false) to them. Now, if you're a Christian, anything that states that Jesus was *not* both God and man is heretical. You see what Paul was trying to address here?

What it Takes:

As you read Colossians, you may not notice something else, but it's crucial: Paul uses the Gnostics' own language to counteract their teaching. For instance, in Colossians 2:9, he uses the term "the fullness of God" when "fullness" was a Gnostic word. Essenes believed "fullness" could not be realized in the physical world. Paul is telling them that the two realms—spiritual and physical—have come together in the person of Christ. It has, thus, been realized! If you watch for it, you'll see that he worded it in a way that would resonate with them through his understanding of their language, teaching, and beliefs.

Because Paul used their language, does this mean he was caving to their culture? Not in the least. He consistently points to and holds to the truth of the Gospel. Then, he doubles down on his message by modeling for us how to live in the world but not of it—to meet people where they're at and point them to Christ. Could we do the same?

How to Get There:

People are paid to influence us these days and we are vulnerable to it. But we have the potential to be influential to those around us as well. Being in this world and not of it looks like humbling ourselves (Phil. 2:1-11) and being lights in the world (Phil. 2:15) for Him. Our behavior, humble attitude, and service of others allow us to stand out as Christians and represent Christ well. Then, we are trusted sources to speak truth into others' lives.

Prayer Points

1. God, how am I allowing myself to be vulnerable to outside influences?

2. How can I influence others biblically before they have the ability to influence me?

3. In what ways do I need to be humbled?

Dig Deeper

Read Colossians 1-4. Recognize what Paul was writing in response to (the influence surrounding them).

WEEK THREE

Seek

DAY FOUR

One Verse

"Let the morning bring me word of your unfailing love, for I have put my trust in you. Show me the way I should go, for to you I entrust my life." Psalm 143:8 (NIV)

There's a definite briskness in the air. I immediately see the fog of my breath. Even with a beanie and gloves on, I am not sure the remaining seventeen minutes outside won't leave my toes numb. In autumn of 2020, on a ministry staff retreat, we drove to Michigan to stay in a cabin for a night, enjoy time away for reflection, and experience some team building. One activity instructed us to take a single verse of Scripture, meditate on it for twenty minutes, and spend some time with God.

One verse. Twenty minutes.

Admittedly, slowing down and shutting up long enough for God to speak to me is difficult. Nevertheless, I grabbed my Bible and did some context digging.

Then I realized I still had seventeen minutes left.

My natural tendency, and what I've spent thousands of dollars learning to do at a university, is to dissect the Bible, taking it apart, and studying it. That wasn't the assignment. I was to sit with it. Meditate on it and pray through it. So, I wrote Psalm 143:8 down and took it with me on a walk. I didn't want to fail at such a simple task, so I read this verse about thirty times. Can you guess what happened?

I accidentally memorized it. I didn't mean to; it truly happened organically. A week later, on my drive to work at the church, the guilt of skipping my morning Bible time hits me. Historically, I've gone to the shame place when this happens, but not this time. I immediately started repeating the Scripture I'd read and reread at the retreat. I meditated on it once again, prayed over it, and had some sweet time with my Savior by connecting and giving my day to Him.

Now, if I had sat down with my Bible earlier that morning, could my connection have been stronger? Sure. But God met me where I was—in my stage of life and in that car.

Why it Matters:

God utilized the Scripture written on my heart.

He showed me the incredible impact of memorizing Scripture. In turn, I felt the nudge to enter a season of intentionally memorizing more verses. I started with memorizing Psalm 143 in its entirety, without knowing the full reason why.

What it Takes:

The story continues tomorrow. For today, meditate and reflect on this Scripture. What a beautiful way to align your heart and mind with His.

"Let the morning bring me word of your unfailing love, for I have put my trust in you. Show me the way I should go, for to you I entrust my life." Psalm 143:8

How to Get There:

How often is meditating on Scripture something you regularly participate in? Try the same practice that I did. Dedicate a chunk of time to meditation and prayer on a specific verse. Use the one above if needed.

Prayer Points

1. Where can I make room to intentionally memorize Scrip-

ture in my day?

2. In what ways has the Holy Spirit been impressing a particular Scripture upon my heart?

3. God, how can I better open up to You and allow You to utilize the Scripture I have memorized already?

Dig Deeper

To prepare for tomorrow, read Psalm 143 entirely. Dig for its context first.

WEEK THREE

seek

DAY FIVE

In Suffering

"Let the morning bring me word of your unfailing love, for I have put my trust in you. Show me the way I should go, for to you I entrust my life." Psalm 143:8

Things were healing just fine from my sinus surgery, until they weren't. A sneezing fit erupted. The blood started pouring out of my nose nonstop, which landed me back at the doctor's office twice that day. They packed my sinuses up and sent me home. My marching orders were simple: sit straight up for the next four to five days. Stay still while the gauze disintegrates into my sinus cavity as the blood vessel heals. I could not start bleeding again.

The enemy tackled my mind that first night as I attempted to sleep. All the fears and the sense of all the ways I was failing my family by being this useless swirled around my brain's front and center. I couldn't cry because that would undoubtedly start the bleeding again, so I was holding it all in. I began to pray, but I only had the capacity to beg God to make the pain stop and not let me bleed to death.

Then, something profound happened. Without realizing it, I started rehearsing the Scripture I'd memorized in the months prior: Psalm 143. It was strange to hear it in my head, my own voice, saying the words over and over suddenly. And do you know what Psalm 143 says?

"Lord, hear my prayer, listen to my cry for mercy;

in your faithfulness and righteousness,

come to my relief.

Do not bring your servant into judgment,

for no one living is righteous before you.

The enemy pursues me,

he crushes me to the ground;

he makes me dwell in the darkness

like those long dead.

So my spirit grows faint within me;

my heart within me is dismayed.

I remember the days of long ago;

I meditate on all your works

and consider what your hands have done.

I spread out my hands to you;

my soul thirst for you like a parched land.

Answer me quickly, Lord;

my spirit fails.

Do not hide your face from me

or I will be like those who go down to the pit.

Let the morning bring me word of your

unfailing love,

for I have put my trust in you.

Show me the way I should go,

for to you I entrust my life."

Psalm 143:1-8 (NIV)

Why It Matters:

God prepared me for this time of suffering. That prayer was every-thing my heart needed to say, and the weight of everything happen-ing began to lift. The Holy Spirit intervened on my behalf.

I could have memorized any Scripture leading up to this day, but that's not how God works; He's intentional. I realize now that God pulled me out of the proverbial "pit" before I even hit it. I started to recognize that if God had prepared me for this time of agony, would He not have prepared my husband and kids to handle everything else?

My first sign of healing followed the first night of actual sleep. I felt the swelling was down, so I turned on the light next to me, revealing the blood covering my shirt. At that moment, I had every reason to unravel, but the truth is that I was calm. My doctor said I needed to go to the hospital immediately, but no one in the ER would have the instrument to repack the gauze. Then he finished with the fact that he had COVID, so they wouldn't let him go in to treat me.

Of course.

With few options in the ER and the bleeding subsiding, the decision was made to stay the course: sit "still-er" and wait. So that's what I did. And slowly, and I mean slowly, I healed.

What it Takes:

The impact of what had just happened was not lost on me. After praying and meditating on these words, "Show me the way I should go, for to you I entrust my life," I started to mean it. God had a purpose, and I *did* trust Him.

That's when it clicked: I didn't utilize the Scripture I had written on my heart; the Holy Spirit did.

How to Get There:

So, the question I've been left with ever since is the question I leave you to ask yourself today: What am I giving the Holy Spirit to work with?

Prayer Points

1. Lord, what Scriptures are written on my heart that You could bring to the surface?

2. What opportunities throughout the day do I have to memorize Scripture in my downtime?

3. God, how have You prepared me for times of suffering or struggle?

Dig Deeper

Make a list of Scriptures you already have memorized. Take today to think about all the situations you're currently facing. What does the Bible have to say about how you are to react or behave? Write verses down and commit to memorizing them. Give the Holy Spirit something to work with.

WEEK THREE

Seek

DAY SIX

Meditating

"For the weapons of our warfare are not of the flesh but have divine power to destroy strongholds. We destroy arguments and every lofty opinion raised against the knowledge of God, and take every thought captive to obey Christ, being ready to punish every disobedience, when your obedience is complete." 2 Corin. 10:4-6

We were all fuming.

A dad on the baseball communication app was chewing out the coaches who spend countless, thankless hours pouring into our kids. Oh, I rehearsed my response. I let the anger build up and made this guy out to be an absolute monster in my head.

I meditated. I meditated on the anger, frustration, and disappointment. I let my emotions fester over all the negative elements of the situation. I felt the enemy laughing at me because all he needed was an inch, and I'd given him a mile.

Why it Matters:

We tend to meditate on the thing that hurt us when, in fact, God calls us to do the exact opposite: "but his delight is in the Law of the Lord, and on his law he meditates day and night." Psalm 1:2

What it Takes:

Picture a different kind of day than the one I just described. Instead of meditating on the anger or the negative toxic emotions, what would happen if instead you took every issue that plagues your life and assaulted it with Scripture?

How about when your child is afraid to go to bed alone in a dark room? You're just exhausted from the nighttime routine dragging out once again. You want to tell them to be quiet. Suddenly, you're prompted with:

"When I am afraid, I put my trust in you, in God, whose Word I praise, in God I trust, I shall not be afraid. What can flesh do to me?" Psalm 56:3-4

So, you choose to cuddle up next to your fearful child and pray this verse with them, instead of letting the annoyance win.

Or imagine what happens amid sin's temptation. Someone says, "You deserve this." Yet you know something isn't quite right. Then you hear this in your spirit:

"No temptation has overtaken you that is not common to man. God is faithful, and he will not let you be tempted beyond your ability, but with the temptation he will also provide the way of escape, that you may be able to endure it." 1 Corinthians 10:13

Or what about that moment when you choose the voice of guilt? You go back to a habit or a relationship that you've been set free from by the grace of God. Then you're reminded:

"For freedom Christ has set us free; stand firm therefore, and do not submit again to a yoke of slavery." Galatians 5:1

And you *do* stand firm instead of letting that habit or person back into your life.

How about in conflict, bubbling with frustration:

"Out of my distress I called on the Lord; the Lord answered me and set me free. The Lord is on my side; I will not fear. What can man do to me?" Psalm 118:5-6

Or while having a conversation with someone about faith, they get combative or disrespectful. You don't know where to take the conversation. But you remember in your heart that Jesus said:

"'So everyone who acknowledges me before men, I also will acknowledge before my Father who is in heaven, but whoever denies me before men, I also will deny before my Father who is in heaven.'" Matthew 10:32-33

So, you stay in the conversation, engage respectfully, and share the love of Christ with them.

Or when you're struggling just to be okay:

"Rejoice always, pray without ceasing, give thanks in all circumstances; for this is the will of God in Christ Jesus for you." 1 Thess. 5:16-18

Imagine the effect this could have on your soul and your psyche. What would it be like to choose to meditate all day long on God's Word, allowing Him to use it and put it to work?

What are you meditating on? What are you giving power to? What are you giving the Holy Spirit to work with?

We have to put Scripture in our hearts if we want it to stay there. Instead of making His Word about us, we're entering it into our lives, taking it with us all day. It's a different approach than the world's way of plucking Scripture from its context and attaching it to life when convenient.

How to Get There:

Today, evaluate your treatment of Scripture and how you want to proceed with it in your life.

Prayer Points

1. What am I meditating on? What am I giving power to?

2. Lord, in what ways does my focus typically turn to You? In what ways does it turn to focusing on the problem?

3. How can I better attach Scripture to my life in a way that honors it?

Dig Deeper

Write out the Scriptures from Day 6 on index cards. Bring them with you throughout your day.

WEEK THREE

Seek

DAY SEVEN

Check-In Day

How am I seeking God's voice by honoring Scripture?

Looking at Scripture this week through a new lens was risky. The goal was not to intimidate you from reading it! Honoring Scripture takes work, practice, and diligence.

It's a treasure we have from God. It's His infallible Word and one of the greatest gifts He's given us. Yes, when we read it without context or cherry-pick verses, we can misconstrue it. That doesn't mean that we don't turn to it just because we don't have an hour to do a deep-dive context study. Open it and ask the Holy Spirit to guide you. The Holy Spirit's presence— another gift from God. We're pretty spoiled.

Whatever your thoughts and feelings about honoring Scripture were this week, take them to Him. Let Him know where you're at and where you want Him to take you. Remember, nothing is off the table when it comes to conversing with Him. Let it out.

Prayer Points

1. Lord, in what ways have I been honoring your Word and applying it well?

2. What parts of Scripture have I misunderstood?

3. When do I turn to Your Word for guidance and when do I turn to worldly resources?

4. How can I better seek Your voice through Your Word?

Memorize

BELIEVE

DECIDE

SEEK

PRAY

LIVE

PRAISE

SHARE

WEEK FOUR

pray

DAY ONE

Pray like Your Life Depends on It

Why do we pray about the same thing hundreds of times if God is going to do His will anyway?

Devastation rips at my heart. I pray for my friend. Over and over, I ask God, "Help my friend ditch addiction and turn to Christ." Yet nothing happens. Nothing has changed in nine, ten or eleven years, so why does God need my 694th prayer?

What if that 694th prayer is the one God uses to change something inside of *me?* What if that's what God plans to use in my friend's life?

Why it Matters:

Prayer tends to be transactional rather than relational, a one-sided conversation where we tell God things and ask for help. Does He want to hear from us? Of course. Scripture tells us He does.

But if we desire to make lasting change in our hearts, we must open ourselves up to a listening posture. How? As you may have noticed these past three weeks, *the power is in the questions.*

What it Takes:

When we ask the right questions, we're forced to be quiet long enough to listen to Him. First, we ask. Then we seek because we are promised we will find (Matt. 7:7-8). This way He can teach us how to live the life we're called to live. He can show us how to glorify Him right where we've been placed.

Picture two sides of a room. On the first side sits a cold, gray metal chair. It's wildly uncomfortable looking and certainly wobbles unevenly on the floor. It feels lonely. It offers nothing more than temporary relief to get off your feet. There's no draw to sit there. Restless, you look around for another solution.

On the second side sits a cozy little bench. Soft, fluffy blankets and throw pillows reside beside an ottoman, perfectly placed to prop feet up on. A hot cup of your very favorite coffee sends its aroma throughout the room. It sits on a table next to a sweet treat. This is the kind of place you go with your best friend. Here, you spend hours catching up with one another as you bear your soul.

It's obvious which side feels more inviting.

These are like the places you might go to in your heart in prayer. The first side with the cold, metal chair represents what we may have done our whole lives. It displays a stark, transactional posture. We may clean up our prayers so they feel presentable to God. We don't desire to stay here long; it's not super comfortable, and we don't enjoy it much. But we're doing it because we know we should.

The thought comes, *"I need to work on my prayer life."* So, we spend more time planted there in that wobbly uncomfortable chair. In reality, we are praying for anything and everything and we automatically trust God will honor our time and effort. The words spoken may sound like this: "God, I'm scared to do what You've called me to do. Please give me courage." Is there anything wrong with those words? Of course not.

On the other hand, what if you scooted over to the inviting bench and took a seat? Throw that blanket up over your toes. Start sipping your coffee. What happens if you take a minute to align your heart with the Person you are speaking to, opening up truthfully? You've likely been here before, most often when a struggle sits heavy on your chest.

Even with the same thing on your heart as before, the words come out differently.

"Hey Lord, me again. So, You've got this thing You want me to do? It's scary. I don't actually know why I'm scared. You've been with me every time You've asked me to do something. Why am I afraid? What's holding me back? Would You reveal to me what's happening in my heart that explains why I'm not resting in You? Could You remind me of Your truth? Lord, what are You doing? Who do You want me to become through this?"

There's power in those questions. They open us up and move us into relationship.

We both know we'll probably head back to that cold metal chair at some point. We'll sit down carefully and feel the chill up our spine from the alarming temperature change in our heart. It's an uncomfortable yet easier solution because we feel we are acting "Christian-y" since we've taken our concerns to God. We check that box off our to-do list.

"God, my marriage is a mess. I ask You to fix it."

Sometimes, these transactional prayers are all we have in us. We go through the motions.

But, when we're ready, we make our way to the inviting bench. Jesus sits there with us, ready to listen, perhaps even reveal something to us. So, safe in this relationship with Him, we risk offering a deeper prayer.

"God, my marriage is a mess. What is going on in my marriage? What is going on in my heart towards my husband? I'm resentful. It affects my entire family. What are You trying to show me about me? I want to be the kind of person You want me to be. I think that might help me be the kind of wife he needs. I'm hurting, God. Help me communicate my true heart to You and to my husband. Please, will You show me what's really going on?"

Then, it becomes easier to go to God in prayer and may even become a habit. We bring things that we didn't really want to go too deep into because we feel safe. We ask about things that used to seem small and not worthy of bringing to Him.

Instead of prayers that state the obvious yet don't go beyond the surface, we get honest. We used to pray like this:

"God, I am so anxious about everything. I can't seem to get my house in order, literally. It's a mess; everywhere I go, I'm exhausted from doing it all, and it never ends. Help."

Now, our prayers hold substance and raw vulnerability.

"God, why am I so anxious about all this? Why do I care so much that everything has to be perfect? Do I just like the control? Who am I trying to impress? What's causing me to rely on a tidy house to bring inner peace? I want to rely on You for that! Father, help me not serve my perfection by how I present things in my house. Reorder me within, God."

Prayer, heart communication with God, expands our soul as we go in a little deeper.

In the metal chair, I pray routine words that don't delve deep.

"God, I'm scared. Please heal this person I love."

On the bench, my prayers unearth what I need to see within me.

"God, I'm terrified and can't stop thinking about this. You haven't healed this person I love, and I am scared I'll lose them. I've lost people before, so isn't it fair to feel this way? I've also seen You heal. I'm not trusting You because I've seen You use tragedy for good.

Typically, I hope my heart's desire is Your will, but now I want my will here. I know You love this friend of mine. I ask for healing, but I also ask that You show me how to rest in Your plans. Could you help me to trust You? Could You help me see why I'm not trusting you? Would you please use this whole thing for Your glory, even if I don't mean it now? Do it Your way, God, even when I want my will more. Whatever You're doing, show me who You need me to be through this."

In this place, God reminds us of His grace. As we bring this to Him, He will honor our desire to follow Him, even when it's not completely pure yet, even when it's still a bit self-serving. And slowly, with Him, He will hone those tendencies to reflect a purer heart.

Transformation happens on the bench where heart-deep dialogue takes place.

It becomes a place we desire so intensely to be with God and hear His voice that we can't wait to return to that type of prayer. We go there before we call our best friend because God becomes the One we want to converse with—not only because He's the One with the power, but also because He's the One who holds our heart.

The power is in the questions. That's where we learn to lay our hearts out honestly and move into a listening posture. Then, as we go throughout our day, we start to see God answer through people, Scripture, sermons, and our own calmness in a situation.

How to Get There:

It's time to head over to the bench.

Prayer Points

1. How have I stayed in the "transactional" prayer category?

2. Lord, what area of my prayer life (my heart) doesn't enjoy time with You?

3. Father, will You show me how to open up more honestly to You? What is holding me back?

Dig Deeper

Read Ephesians 4:22-24. How is this a transformation you desire? Take this to God in honest prayer.

WEEK FOUR

pray

DAY TWO

Ugly Prayers

"Who can discern his errors? Declare me innocent from hidden faults. Keep back your servant also from presumptuous sins; let them not have dominion over me! Then I shall be blameless, and innocent of great transgression. Let the words of my mouth and the meditation of my heart be acceptable in your sight, O LORD, my Rock and my Redeemer." Psalm 19:12-14

"He never dealt with the trauma." This was the cry of a girlfriend after a rough breakup. The guy was not only angry, but he went so far as to manifest problems out of thin air. He made up lies about her with absolutely no basis. He pushed her away while lashing out, displaying an adult tantrum.

Why It Matters:

Our past tends to creep in on us when we least expect it. Her boyfriend's past trauma never received the healing it needed. It turned and became hurtful to her years later. We can't overlook the impact difficult parts of our past have on those around us.

We have to deal with it.

We like to poke fun at the Israelites for grumbling in Exodus and Numbers. They sounded so dramatic out in the desert, whining from Day One that God brought them out into the miserable desert to starve them to death.

Their past is controlling the moment at hand and their attitude. They'd been hungry before, so they're worried it will happen again. They've seen loved ones die, so they don't believe everyone is going to live.

They are having a hard time trusting.

Can you think of a time that felt like it was hard to trust? Can you better relate to their thoughts? We've been burned, so we don't connect. We've been hurt, so we don't open up. We've been abandoned, neglected, mistreated, you name it, and we don't deal with it. And who does it affect? Those we love most. Our loved ones deal with the aftermath that occurs through our anger and mistrust, through walls we've put up around our hearts.

We can't overcome these deep, lifelong hurts by ourselves. We have to pray our way through them with the One who has the power to enact true change in our hearts.

What it Takes:

I was led to read three Psalms: Psalm 6, Psalm 38, and Psalm 42. If you want to see ugly emotions up close, these authors held nothing back. Listen in:

"I am weary with my moaning; every night I flood my bed with tears; I drench my couch with my weeping. My eye wastes away because of grief; it grows weak because of all my foes." Psalm 6:6-7

"My wounds stink and fester because of my foolishness, I am utterly bowed down and prostrate; all the days I go about mourning. For my sides are filled with burning, and there is no soundness in my flesh. I am feeble and crushed; I groan because of the tumult in my heart." Psalm 38:5-8

"I say to God my Rock, 'Why have you forgotten me? Why must I go about mourning, oppressed by the enemy?' My bones suffer mortal agony as my foes taunt me, saying to me all day long, 'Where is your God?'" Psalm 42:9-10

These psalmists bring their anguish and doubt to God. I must be honest. I don't often feel worthy to complain as deeply as the authors in these Psalms do. I hold back the stuff I pretend He doesn't know about—the dark stuff, the ugly prayers.

How to Get There:

So, my question for you today is: how raw do your prayers get? Does your Father, your Creator, the One who knows you better than yourself, does He get all that's within you?

He already knows. He wants to take all the trauma and hurt you haven't dealt with and not allow it to continue to hurt you and those around you. He wants to stop the cycle. What will you need to shift to allow Him to do that?

Prayer Points

> 1. Father, how am I being honest with You in my prayers?
>
> 2. What am I holding back from You?
>
> 3. How am I not trusting You with the hard stuff?

Dig Deeper

Check out Psalm 6, Psalm 38, and Psalm 42. Take some of that ugly stuff within you to the One who's already wiped it away and planned a better tomorrow for you, the one He loves. And the ones you love.

WEEK FOUR

pray

DAY THREE

Shame

"Prayer is not a place to be good, it is a place to be honest. Prayer is not a place to perform; it is a place to be present. Prayer is not a place to be right, it is a place to be known. Prayer is not a place to prove your worth, it is a place to receive worth and offer yourself in truth.[11] —*Where Prayer Becomes Real: How Honesty with God Transforms Your Soul*, Kyle Strobel

How quickly do you hold your head in shame after sinful behavior? That's my go-to place: shame. I distance myself from God as if I'm not worthy to talk to Him, as though I need to clean up my life before coming to Him.

That's not His design.

"When you're convicted of sin, what do you do with it?"[12]Think about this because it can only end in two ways: Does it bring you to God, or does it take you to yourself?

I'm curious if you do what I've done. I take what I messed up and fix it to the absolute best of my ability.

My ability.

Why it Matters:

Shame says we take our righteousness on ourselves, but righteousness doesn't come from us. As the Gospel of John explains, "Abide in me, and I in you. As the branch cannot bear fruit by itself, unless it abides in the vine, neither can you, unless you abide in me." John 15:4

What it Takes:

When we truly choose to abide in Him, He can produce righteousness through us. This requires an overhauling of our prayer life. It's not that we're to try harder. We're to give more of ourselves to Him.

Shame from something we've done says we've taken our righteousness on ourselves. Essentially, our transformation depends on us. It just is not the way things work.

"And I am sure of this, that he who began a good work in you will bring it to completion at the day of Jesus Christ." Phil. 1:6

How to Get There:

So, the question we are going to wrestle with today is this:

"Am I bringing God the shame I feel (after the fact), or am I bringing God the sin, the honest ongoing issue?"

Grace allows me to bring the sin.

Prayer Points

1. God, in what ways do I bring You my ongoing sin?

2. In what ways do I bring You remorse and shame after the sin has already occurred?

3. When it comes to the most significant areas of shame in my life, what would it look like to bring You the sin before it happens? How can you re-train that area of my heart away from sin?

Dig Deeper

Today's devotion was short and sweet to give you time to read Psalm 51. Start with an understanding of where David was in his life. Notice what he brought to God. Do some research to find out the context details.

WEEK FOUR

pray

DAY FOUR

He Can

"Now to him who is able to do far more abundantly than all that we ask or think, according to the power at work within us, to him be glory in the church and in Christ Jesus throughout all generations, forever and ever. Amen." Ephesians 3:20-21

"How can we pray 'in faith' for healing? Are we supposed to pray with absolute confidence that God will heal? What about when He doesn't heal? Does that mean I didn't have enough faith? Am I being punished when things don't get better?"

Our Bible study headed into a rabbit hole conversation that made my mind reel. These heavy questions provoked us to search our minds and hearts for everything we'd ever learned about God! I desperately wanted to reassure everyone with truth from God's Word. Amidst the pain and suffering many shared, I wasn't sure how to be an encouragement. Then, as all our thoughts started spinning, a friend quieted the room with two words:

"He Can."

That's all she said, and that's all we needed.

Why it Matters:

We have faith that *He can*. We continue our praise because *He can*. We continue in faith because *He can*. We continue to trust <u>not with the stipulation that He will</u> but because *He can*.

So, we go to Him in prayer, believing *He can*, then ask in faith that He does—sometimes begging in faith that He does. This becomes the foundation we stand on, no matter the outcome.

What it Takes:

This requires a decision. Is your faith bigger than your pain, bigger than your suffering, and bigger than watching someone you love suffer? This is hard to live out, brutal even. It requires us to pray with a trusting heart, with full-blown surrender.

Paul says, "Now to him who is able to do far more abundantly than all that we ask or think, according to the power at work within us..." (Ephesians 3:20)

It's trusting that God is able to do more than we can grasp. Often, we don't know what God is doing or why. Once again, we choose to trust in His perfect providence and tell Him so.

How to Get There:

Spend some extra time in prayer today. Trust that if you want to go deeper in your relationship with God, He will go there with you. Tell Him where you're at and where you want to be.

Prayer Points

1. God, where is my foundation of trust in You strong enough to withstand whatever comes?

2. How am I trusting You in my current situation?

3. How am I trusting You in my relationships?

4. In what ways am I holding back, not trusting You?

5. Lord, in what ways is my trust in You filled with stipulations attached?

Dig Deeper

Romans 5:3-4 says, "Not only that, but we rejoice in our sufferings, knowing that suffering produces endurance, and endurance produces character, and character produces hope."

- How do these verses give you hope or frustrate you? Take either answer to God in prayer.

WEEK FOUR

pray

DAY FIVE

His Purpose

"Now to him who is able to do far more abundantly than all that we ask or think, according to the power at work within us, to him be glory in the church and in Christ Jesus throughout all generations, forever and ever. Amen." Ephesians 3:20-21

I'm very protective of God's feelings. Don't worry; it sounds just as ridiculous in my head as it sounds on paper. But this is the conclusion I've arrived at, based on evaluating my prayer life. I don't want to hurt God's feelings. If I let Him into certain parts of my heart and soul that aren't so pretty or into areas where my faith isn't so strong, I think I will disappoint Him.

Talk about a holy conviction. I know better.

Take a moment and reflect on what you typically pray for. Ever pray about the future? My husband and I are both dreamers. The comical thing is that we're dreamers in entirely different ways.

He's practical and reasonable, but his plans constantly change based on circumstances. Then, he must restructure every detail and rethink the next five years. On the contrary, I like to see the outcome completed in my head and groan as I work out the details.

Why it Matters:

We all dream and plan our lives. God has given us unique talents and incredible brains and expects us to utilize them all. But for what purpose?

Romans 8:28 often gets thrown around as an explanation for everything, and for good reason. But when you chew on this verse slowly, the main point becomes more apparent. "And we know that in all things God works for the good of those who love him, who have been called according to *His* purpose." God's purpose must remain at the forefront, or all is null and void. When we attach this verse to our lives with *our* purpose in mind, we aren't honoring its intent and, thus, not honoring God.

What it Takes:

If we abide in Him as John 15:4 tells us, then our genuine desires begin to align with God's desires. Our opinion on our life starts to matter less and less as we train ourselves to surrender to His desire. Yes, we can train ourselves to turn to Him, lean on Him, and trust Him. Yes, this is the same verse as yesterday. Lots to unpack here!

Ephesians 3:20-21 says, "Now to him who is able to do far more abundantly than all that we ask or think, according to the power at work within us, to him be glory in the church and in Christ Jesus throughout all generations, forever and ever. Amen"

He is able to do more.

How to Get There:

What if we surrendered everything to Him today? Then, we get to be a part of His plan. Instead of letting God know your plans today and for the future, take a moment and ask Him what He has in mind first.

Prayer Points

1. God, what do You need me to accomplish today? How can I be open to those You send my way, and how can I bless them?

2. Today, how can I surrender my plans and my dreams to You? I ask Your will to be done in every situation, ahead of my own will.

3. Lord, what needs to change in my heart to desire Your plans over my own plans?

Dig Deeper

Read Romans 8:9-30. Rest in the promise of eternity to come.

WEEK FOUR

pray

DAY SIX

Warriors

"And we prayed to our God and set a guard as a protection against them day and night." Nehemiah 4:9

What's it like to fight emotionally for yourself or the people you take care of? This place wears us out. I've become increasingly aware of the effects of emotional exhaustion this past year. I still know God is there, so I pray, ask for His strength, and request all kinds of things, but I still feel just weak and tired. How are we supposed to fight?

Why it Matters:

The rebuilding of the wall in Jerusalem was a monstrous task that Nehemiah undertook, especially with opposition coming at them from enemy forces. The Jews all worked hard at first then became immensely frustrated. "Their strength was giving out....and the enemy was ready to attack." (Nehemiah 4:10,12)

Do you see the spiritual correlation here?

"From that day on, half of my servants worked on construction, and half held the spears, shields, bows and coats of mail. And the leaders stood behind the whole house of Judah, who were building on the wall. Those who carried burdens were loaded in such a way that each labored on the work with one hand and held his weapon with the other. " Nehemiah 4:16-17

What does this tell us? Verse 9 gives us insight into our weapon. "And we prayed to our God and set a guard as a protection against them day and night."

Who are you positioning around you to stand guard and pray on your behalf? It's hard to tell those around you that you're struggling, especially when you know you have a blessed life. Yet, in case no one has told you, the people who love you want in. They want to know your heart and how they can pray for you. Have you ever asked someone who loves you to pray for you? Did they ever say no?

What it Takes:

You need prayer warriors—others who can fight for you when you can't fight for yourself. That's the first thing these guys with Nehemiah did. They prayed, then devoted half their men to standing guard and held a sword in one hand 24/7.

The enemy wants control. He wants to control our emotions, focus, and joy. He wants it all, and we often position him to take it all by being vulnerable to his tactics. Prayer combats all of that.

How to Get There:

Make sure you're covered on all sides. You need prayer. There is no shame in asking for it.

Prayer Points

1. Lord, who have You positioned around me to pray on my behalf?

2. Who else could I trust with my prayer requests that could battle in prayer for me?

3. How can I better open up to those I trust and ask for prayer?

Dig Deeper

Read Ephesians 6:18-20. Note how Paul asks these individuals to pray for him. What is he always pointing to?

WEEK FOUR

pray

DAY SEVEN

Check-In Day

How am I praying like my life depends on it?

Max Lucado says, "Our prayers may be awkward. Our attempts may be feeble. But since the power of prayer is in the One who hears it and not in the one who says it, our prayers do make a difference."[13]

While teaching the spiritual formation class, Dr. John Coe gave four prayers for us to say to start every day. When I am faithful to say them, my entire day shifts.

Here's my challenge to you. Write them down. Pray them now. Pray them every morning for the next week. See what God does within you.

Prayer Points:

Prayer of Intentions

1. "God, I am here. I present myself to You." (Romans 12:1-2, presenting oneself as a living sacrifice)

2. "God, whatever I do today, I want to do this in You. I don't want to do this alone, in my own power, or as a way to hide and cover. I don't want to find my identity in anything else but Christ."

3. "Lord, what is going on in my heart right now with You, with others, with my life, with my situations? Open my heart to You today in trust, lest I deceive myself."

4. "Lord, what are You doing and what is it You want me to become and do if I am to do Your will?"[14]

Memorize

BELIEVE

DECIDE

SEEK

PRAY

LIVE

PRAISE

SHARE

WEEK FIVE

live

DAY ONE

Live Life God's Way

My chickens teach me profound lessons. In January in Indiana, an arctic blast froze the earth around here. When the weather drops so drastically, I'm always tempted to get out the heat lamp for the chickens because I cannot imagine that there's any way those feathered creatures will survive. However, as a chicken owner, I learned two main things about their winter survival.

First, the chickens' water supply is crucial. Pretty simple to remember.

Second, they need to feather out to maintain warmth in freezing temperatures. If I give them a heat lamp, they wouldn't feather out. If they don't feather out and the heat lamp goes out at any point, there's a high probability they will die without protection from the extra warmth. God designed chickens in such a way that their bodies provide what they need to survive. Going against God's design by introducing a heat lamp could kill them.

When I bundled up and walked down to their coup on that cold January 16th day, lo and behold, they were fine—thriving even. Because I honored God's design.

Why it Matters:

Galatians 5:16-17 doesn't say anything about chickens, but it does say this:

"But I say, walk by the Spirit, and you will not gratify the desires of the flesh. For the desires of the flesh are against the Spirit, and the desires of the Spirit are against the flesh, for these are opposed to each other, to keep you from doing the things you want to do."

God has a design for us: to walk in the Spirit. Since we are born spiritually dead (which means without the presence of God), we are born with a void in us that only God can fill. Everyone attempts fill the void God created yet He created it for Himself because we are meant to be molded by the Holy Spirit.

Here's the problem. If we are not formed by God, then our spirit (soul, heart) is formed by whatever we place in front of it. The great theologian James Montgomery Boice said,

"The world's theology is easy to define. It is the view that human beings are basically good, that no one is really lost, that belief in Jesus Christ is not necessary for salvation."[15]

The world's theology is scary.

What it Takes:

It's safe to say we need to do two things. First, we need to make sure *the world* is not what our spirit is modeled after. In his book *Mere Christianity*, C.S. Lewis says,

"A world of nice people, content in their own niceness, looking no further, (and) turned away from God, would be just as desperately in need of salvation as a miserable world—and might even be more difficult to save."[16]

Second, we must decide our goal in the Christian life. Are we aiming to simply be nice people? Or is our desire to walk with Christ and allow Him, by His grace to grant us righteousness?

How to Get There:

Start this week by having a real, honest conversation with God about your relationship with Him. Discuss where and how you are living with the Spirit contrary to living by the flesh.

Prayer Points

1. God, what is my goal in my relationship with You?

2. In what ways am I genuinely walking in the Spirit? How am I living without the Spirit's leading?

3. How have I been living my life? Am I striving to be a nice person or striving to walk in the Spirit?

Dig Deeper

Read Galatians 5. Pay attention to the correlation between freedom and walking in the Spirit.

WEEK FIVE

live

DAY TWO

Burnt Out

"I, therefore, a prisoner for the Lord, urge you to walk in a manner worthy of the calling to which you have been called." Ephesians 4:1

Raise your hand if you've felt burnt out at some point in the last year: physically, emotionally, mentally, spiritually. I imagine that includes most of us. We can talk all day long about protecting and respecting ourselves, but none of that will matter unless we establish something else first: so what if we get burnt out and run down? Just take a nap, rally, and get it together. The world around us encourages that mentality.

Why it Matters:

Instead, let's pivot.

In this season of your life, what do you believe your calling is?

I've listened to the hearts of women in all different stages of life. The sweet, tired friend who feels she can barely keep her head above water while surrounded by babies and toddlers, hiding the spit up on her shirt, just trying to survive the day. The smiling grandmother joyfully exhausted, attempts to keep up with all those beautiful grandbabies. The 40-something woman, living in the world of afternoon-and-evening chauffeur duty for multiple kids, food wrappers all over the van floor, dripping in guilt that they haven't had a family dinner in weeks. The ambitious girl you watched grow up who just graduated from college, energized and ready for the real world. The single one rocking her career. The doe-eyed one who just got married or remarried. Do you know what they all have in common?

God has a purpose for them in this stage of their life.

How do I know this? Because otherwise they wouldn't be alive and breathing. The same goes for you: if you are still here on this earth, He has a purpose for your life. Your job is to guard it with everything you've got.

And you are no good to His purpose burnt out.

It's so easy to get caught up in doing good things—great things even—but things we were not called to do. I'm right there with you, too.

What it Takes:

When it comes to defending ourselves from burnout, we have to protect ourselves from two things: *ourselves* and others. In Ephesians 4, Paul tells the Jews and Gentiles to "live a life worthy of the calling you have received." Paul does this thing in all his writing, and it's amazing: He points us to Jesus.

Jesus, too, had a calling on his life. Let's look at his behavior. He didn't heal everyone who asked to be healed; He was purposeful. When He did heal, He often asked the person to do something, like "Get up, take up your bed, and walk" (John 5:8), or even, "see that you say nothing to anyone, but go, show yourself to the priest and offer the gift that Moses commanded, for a proof to them." (Matt 8:4).

Notice how Jesus valued His physical body. When He returned to earth after the resurrection, he went to the Sea of Galilee and ate which proves He was the same human they knew and loved. This also affirms that humans have physical needs. Jesus didn't overdo His capacity by revealing Himself to everyone at once. Instead, He stopped for a bit and cared for His human needs. He could love people well since He was in this state of having cared for Himself.

In His time with the disciples, He took naps, went for walks, confided in friends (Matt 26:36-38), and made prayer an absolute priority without feeling guilty. Because of this, He was rested, well-nourished, and prayed up when the enemy tempted Him. Jesus was well enough to handle life when it hit.

God invites you to be a good steward of your own body, too. In Matthew 11:30, Jesus said, "My yoke is easy and my burden is light." So consider these questions: How's your burden? Where are you in danger of burnout? Who cares if you get burnt out?

God does. He needs you to acknowledge your limitations and rely on Him so you can be a part of everything He has planned for your good and His glory.

Burning ourselves out isn't a badge of honor; it's an indicator that we're trying to do life without God's help.

How to Get There:

Jesus modeled servanthood while maintaining boundaries for His own physical body. He proactively protected Himself from burnout to achieve God's purpose.

Jesus prayed from a place of surrender, and God led.

Prayer Points

1. God, what do You need me to do? Remind me daily to surrender my schedule to You.

2. What are You going to take care of without me?

3. Where am I failing to place a boundary of care for my phys-

ical body?

Dig Deeper

Read Matthew 11:25-30. Reflect today on how this applies to your life.

WEEK FIVE

live

DAY THREE

Vanilla Lasagna

"Each of you should use whatever gift you have received to serve others, as faithful stewards of God's grace in its various forms." 1 Peter 4:10

A few years ago, my children were in the crawling-baby stage. I found it increasingly hard to consistently show up anywhere outside of the home. I still wanted to serve and see other humans, so I decided to make meals for people who had babies or were sick. I thought maybe, just maybe, I possessed the gift of hospitality.

The first meal I planned to make was a pot roast. Throw it in a crock pot. How could I possibly get it wrong? Well, I decided to put the whole crock pot in my car to transport the meal. (No, it didn't have a sealing lid on it). There were bumps. Need I say more? My car smelled like pot roast for the better part of a month. Thoroughly annoyed with myself, the whole ordeal frustrated me for the rest of the day.

Strike One.

Then, a family we knew gave birth to twins; it was time to redeem myself. I decided on a chicken-and-rice casserole. Since you always make two recipes, keeping one for yourself, I made a terrible discovery as our family sat down to dinner. Every bite felt as if we were going to break our teeth. I purchased the wrong kind of rice. So, I had to call the father of newborn twins and tell him how to attempt to salvage the meal.

Strike Two.

Then, I remembered my old-faithful dish: lasagna. It's my own recipe created with Greek yogurt to add a healthy boost. How could I possibly mess up my familiar, reliable recipe? I dropped the meal off and came home to put ours in the oven. As I opened the fridge to grab another item, my eyes land on the container of Greek yogurt.

Fun fact: At the grocery store, *plain* Greek yogurt sits on the shelf right next to *vanilla* Greek yogurt. Vanilla lasagna??? Oh, no.

Strike Three.

Why it Matters:

None of this gave me any joy. I wanted to serve. I needed to find my place in the church, but I wasn't there quite yet.

"As each has received a gift, use it to serve one another, as good stewards of God's varied grace: whoever speaks, as one who speaks oracles of God; whoever serves, as one who serves by the strength that God supplies—in order that in everything God may be glorified through Jesus Christ. To him belong glory and dominion forever and ever. Amen." 1 Peter 4:10-11

What it Takes:

When I saw others in the church serving in various ways with joy, I wanted to do the same thing. So, I started on a journey toward discovering my own spiritual gifting.

Every time church doors open, someone must turn on the lights and set up tables so conversations and fellowship can take place. Someone must pick worship songs, practice, and show up to sing on stage so we can worship. Greeters show up early and stand at the door so a guest who hasn't been to church in twenty years gets a warm welcome and that leads to the courage to step inside.

So, I kept trying. Two elders utilized their gifts of encouragement and wisdom. They suggested I have coffee with our new pastor's wife. These two elders wouldn't let this idea go! So, I met the pastor's wife, who planted a seed in my mind. A yearly retreat was born. Hundreds of women have attended.

I teach now also. Nothing in the church has given me greater joy than teaching and encouraging other women in their walk with God. It's changed my life.

1 Peter 4:10 reads, "Each has received a gift." The Greek word used here for "gift" is *charisma* or its plural *charismata*. The word charismata comes from two shorter words: one is *charis*, meaning "grace." That word charis can be broken down to a shorter word *char*, which means "joy." So *char* is joy, *charis* is "grace," and *charismata* is "gift."[17]

What all that means is there is an inseparable link between joy, grace, and gifting. The Bible says when we receive the *charis*, the grace of God through Jesus Christ, with that grace comes a *charisma*, a spiritual gift. And when we exercise that gift, we experience *char*, true joy and fulfillment in life.

So, if you're going to make a vanilla lasagna, do yourself and the rest of us a favor and don't. Then, you'll have the time and energy to find what God made you to do, something that will serve His church well and bring joy and fulfillment to your heart.

How to Get There:

Instead of *doing* for the sake of doing, seek Him. Ask God where you're gifted, where He needs you, and how to serve Him well.

Prayer Points

 1. God, how can I truly explore the gifts You've given me?

2. Where have I found joy in serving Your church? Where have I lost joy in serving Your church?

3. Where have You given me a gift or talent which I haven't used yet to serve You?

Dig Deeper

Read Romans 12:3-8. Consider your gifting and how you are using it in the body of Christ.

WEEK FIVE

live

DAY FOUR

Personal Boundaries

"He went to him and bound up his wounds, pouring on oil and wine. Then he set him on his own animal and brought him to an inn and took care of him. And the next day he took out two denarii and gave them to the innkeeper, saying, 'Take care of him, and whatever more you spend, I will repay you when I come back'" Luke 10:34-35

You've met that woman with weak boundaries: she's overwhelmed. Her to-do list grows. She says yes when she needs to say no. She's a fixer. Her hands are in everything despite repeatedly falling into burnout. Eventually, this woman will become so emotionally depleted that she will be unable to help or care for others anymore because she's given too much of herself.

Maybe she's you.

Why it Matters:

We need to talk about burnout and battle it because this lack of boundaries opens us up to sin. We all find ourselves doing things in our power that God didn't call us to do. Talking about it feels frustrating and borderline depressing, so what's the point?

The point is there's hope.

Jesus gives such a great example of practicing boundaries when He tells the story of The Parable of the Good Samaritan in Luke 10:25-37. This story has a lot of levels and takeaways. If you look at the Samaritan's behavior, you'll notice something perfectly applicable to this topic.

Let's set the scene: a Jewish man journeys from Jerusalem to Jericho, a 17-mile trek including a descent from 2,500 feet above sea level to 800 feet below sea level. It's desert country. Rocks line the landscape. Quite desolate and so remote that it's an easy environment for robbers to take advantage of people. There's no surprise when the traveler gets robbed, then beaten up. He's injured. He's left alone and will probably die unless someone helps.

Both a priest and a Levite pass by and do nothing, but the Samaritan stops and helps the man.

Let's consider the discord between Jews and Samaritans. Well, their discord is intense. Like, they really hate each other. To let it sink in, picture somebody you don't particularly like (preferably not a person super close to you, for this example). Recall someone you genuinely have no respect for, remembering how something they do offends you; someone you would never call on if you were in trouble, not today, not tomorrow, not even in a million years. This is how these two groups of people felt about each other.

The fact that the man was a Samaritan was a huge deal! The hatred between Jews and Samaritans went back 800 years. Never mind the fact that the priest shunned this guy and went on his way. Never mind the fact that the Levite walked away and did absolutely nothing to help the dying man. (You think Jesus was trying to prove a point?) Yet the man's nemesis came to his aid. These people were taught to hate each other their whole lives.

Taught to hate.

What it Takes:

The Samaritan chose not to hate. But he also did something else: he put boundaries in place.

He was obedient in his call to love others, but he did it in a way that didn't sink him. He did it in a way that set aside his own personal feelings and chose to honor God.

He gave the injured man his "treasure" and took care of him, but he did not give the man all his time. Why? Because he didn't have all his time to give. What if he had? What if he had stayed with him for two months and then lost his job and his family, all out of guilt, because he felt bad?

Did he stay and talk to the man about his feelings? Sure, for one night, to get him set up—then he left. He went to do his job, the job that was paying for the man's care.

We are held to the same standard to love others. However, Jesus shows us that it doesn't have to sink us.

How to Get There:

As we decide what to say yes to, let's take a minute to pause. Take a breath and spend some time in prayer. Ask God to show us where He needs us and, dare we say, where He doesn't!

He can help us learn to protect our personal boundaries, honor the body and life God gave us, and submit to His way of doing things.

Prayer Points

1. God, when I say yes in this current situation, what am I saying no to?

2. What is on my schedule that I'm doing out of guilt?

3. Where can I put better boundaries in place?

Dig Deeper

Read the Parable of the Good Samaritan with this perspective, watching his behavior and the boundaries he kept.

WEEK FIVE

live

DAY FIVE

Relationship Boundaries

"The Lord God took the man and put him in the Garden of Eden to work it and keep it. And the Lord God commanded the man, saying, 'You may surely eat of every tree of the garden; but of the tree of the knowledge of good and evil you shall not eat, for in the day that you eat of it you shall surely die.'" Gen 2:15-17

Boundaries preserve freedom.

Adam and Eve had a great life; God designed it that way. He intended for them to have freedom in the Garden of Eden. He only put one boundary in place: don't eat from the tree of the knowledge of good and evil.

Why it Matters:

The reason for the boundary was to preserve Adam and Eve's freedom.

They could have lived this "good" life forever without evil. Once they ate the restricted fruit, they knew the difference between good and evil by introducing sin into the world. Out of God's great love, He allowed the choice to break the boundary.

And what happened? They rebelled, and sin entered the world. Next thing we know, they're blaming each other for their downfalls, inviting sin into the first human relationship. So, sin enters the world and then immediately starts destroying relationships.

We have boundaries set between us all: the place where you end and I begin. They keep us safe. Good boundaries allow us to be healthy enough to love others well. Well-known therapist Bill Gaultiere puts it like this when he says,

"Good boundaries help you to care for others because you have a stable foundation to operate from and are not distracted or depleted by personal insecurities or blind spots."[18]

C.S. Lewis says,

"Finally, must we not teach that if the home is to be a means of grace it must be a place of rules? ...the alternative to rule is not freedom but the unconstitutional (and often unconscious) tyranny of the most selfish member."[19]

So, if appropriate boundaries are not in place for each member within the structure of a home, the most selfish member wins, i.e. the toddler, the domineering husband, the controlling/nagging wife, or the out-of-control teenager. It's most frustrating when we realize we've let it go on too long. In our minds, it's too far gone.

Yet there is still hope because God's not done. And there's another caveat to the story: if your identity is found in Christ, your relationships should not have the pressure or burden to fulfill you. Don't hear this wrong: you and your feelings matter. However, we must battle this in a godly way if we want actual change. We must follow the example set before us in the Bible.

God shows us this within the Trinity. God, Son, and the Holy Spirit have always been completely fulfilled in each other. Only then did God create us. Therefore, He does not place the burden on us to fulfill Him. Since we're not God, our relationships with humans aren't the same as that of the Trinity. It all comes back to His design: we were created to be fulfilled by God. That's good news! That's freedom from placing a burden on our relationships to fulfill us. We keep our relationships in their proper place and honor God's design for them.

In turn, conflict and hurt can exist in your relationships. These can be resolved by not placing expectations on a person to be something that only God can be; to fill a hole inside of you that only He can fill. That's more good news.

What it Takes:

When did we stop teaching others how to treat us? Boundaries in relationships are for that purpose. To honor God's design for relationships, we keep relationships in their proper place, creating boundaries, so He can give us a small slice of the freedom He designed us to have in the Garden of Eden.

It is unnecessary to lose yourself in your relationships.

How to Get There:

Remember Jesus' perfect example of setting boundaries. Keep re-reading the Gospels and note every time He honored His body and His time. We have the privilege of studying Jesus' life. We study His perfect example of teaching people how to treat us. We can do things God's way by honoring what He's given us and by seeking Him.

Prayer Points

1. God, how am I placing unnecessary expectations on my relationships?

2. How can I better teach people how to treat me?

3. Which of my relationships need better boundaries?

Dig Deeper

Read Genesis 2 and 3. Watch how quickly sin began to affect relationships. What could they have done differently in their relationship to prevent this downfall?

WEEK FIVE

live

DAY SIX

We need to get Webster a Bible

"If you were of the world, the world would love you as its own; but because you are not of the world, but I chose you out of the world, therefore the world hates you." John 15:19

I felt irritated with my trusty old dictionary this past week. As we were doing devotions with my boys, we came across Matthew 5:5 from the Beatitudes, which says, "Blessed are the meek, for they shall inherit the earth."

My son asked what it means to be "meek." My husband and I explained from a biblical perspective, offering my stepdad as an example.

I said, "Grandpa is what Jesus would consider meek. He doesn't just talk to hear himself talk like some of the rest of us do. But when he does talk, you want to shut up to hear what he has to say because it's typically full of wisdom, or it's just funny!"

They laughed. They immediately understood because they know Grandpa. My children know how he carries himself and how he makes them feel. They know his humble and selfless nature. They've seen him sacrifice for others and have watched him go out of his way to do things for them.

Why it Matters:

A couple of days later, I grabbed my dictionary and was alarmed by what it said. When Noah Webster authored the first American dictionary, his goal was to help us understand what a word means. According to my Merriam-Webster dictionary, meek is defined as quiet, gentle, easily imposed on, and submissive.[20]

Jesus was described as meek, but He was no pushover. He wasn't swayed by outside sources or even the devil himself. This definition is flat-out unbiblical.

The biblical description of meek is different: humble, a calm temper, not easily provoked, not self-serving. Humility. Others-focused. Selfless.

What it Takes:

It's comical I am surprised by how the world views the way Jesus calls us to be. Yet this is typical, isn't it? The world misconstrues words all the time, and the world misconstrues Christians all the time.

We are not to be of this world.

John 15:19 says, "If you were of the world, it would love you as its own; but because you are not of the world, but I chose you out of the world, therefore the world hates you."

Striving to be understood or accepted by the world is in vain. Our expectation of ourselves should not be to fit in with the world because we are called to be different.

How to Get There:

Rest in today's process of sanctification. Allow God to work in your heart, molding it to be more like Him.

Prayer Points

1. In what areas of my life am I striving to be accepted and understood by others? How is this keeping me from being more like Christ every day?

2. How can my focus be better centered on You?

3. In what areas of my life am I letting the world influence my opinion of myself and my perspective on life?

Dig Deeper

Read the Beatitudes in Matthew 5 with fresh eyes. Consider how the
world views these characteristics.

WEEK FIVE

live

DAY SEVEN

Check-In Day

How am I living life God's way?

As Christians, we are not in the business of self-help because, as Psalm 121:2 reminds us, that isn't where our help comes from . We humans, though, love control. We get good at managing a lot of things, but our capacity is more limited than we often admit. Outside voices tend to speak lies into our hearts. We find ourselves burnt out, worn out, and useless. Have you recognized this week that this isn't God's design for you?

We can go through all the steps in these seven weeks, yet we will fall on our faces and fail again and again if we miss this one, so take time today to ensure you've walked through this with Him. Releasing control of your own way of life may seem difficult, but it's the most freeing thing you can do.

Prayer Points

1. What area of my life am I overdoing my capacity?

2. God, how am I honoring You with my body and the stress I take on?

3. How am I misunderstanding Your design for my life?

4. How am I walking in the Spirit?

5. How am I not walking in the Spirit?

Memorize

BELIEVE

DECIDE

SEEK

PRAY

LIVE

PRAISE

SHARE

(Come on, make up an obnoxious little song. You can do it. Trust me, you'll want to memorize these!)

WEEK SIX

praise

DAY ONE

Show Praise through a Grateful Attitude

"And let the peace of Christ rule in your hearts, to which indeed you were called in one body. And be thankful. Let the word of Christ dwell in you richly, teaching and admonishing one another in all wisdom, singing psalms and hymns and spiritual songs, with thankfulness in your hearts to God. And whatever you do, in word or deed, do everything in the name of the Lord Jesus, giving thanks to God the Father through him" Colossians 3:15-17

Why it Matters:

This week, we take a step back amid everything you've discovered with God. How many people have you met who walk around with a sour attitude? We can't have absolute trust in God, then let Him lead our lives, honor Scripture as our life's guide, prioritize prayer, and do life God's way if we are still walking around with an ungrateful spirit. This week isn't just about being grateful; it's about a grateful heart.

What is the true meaning of gratitude? Is it simply being thankful? Gratitude is understood as the quality of being grateful and thankful; interest in showing appreciation for <u>and returning kindness.</u>

Don't miss the implication here: gratitude requires *response*.

What it Takes:

Gratitude is not merely being thankful; it's doing something about it. A state of gratitude is *not* simply going through your day thanking everyone for everything they do. Gratitude is treating those around you with love and kindness *out of response* and appreciation for the true gift that they are to you.

When we are truly grateful, we want to do something about it.

This is how we live a life that honors Christ: *out of response* to what He's done for us! As Christians, we discover, at some point along the way, that we desire to follow Him. We desire to rid our lives of sin. We desire to represent Him well when we consider all He's done for us. We do it out of gratitude.

When we look at returning kindness as part of the act and pair that with the last verse above, we have a game plan: "And whatever you do, whether in word or deed, do it all in the name of the Lord Jesus, giving thanks to God the Father through him." (Col. 3:17)

Living out gratitude goes against human nature because of sin. From the Israelites in the desert to the Jews who saw Jesus in the flesh, humans have been good at one thing since the fall: grumbling.

How to Get There:

John 6:43 says, "Jesus answered them, 'Do not grumble among yo urselves.'" Despite Jesus' explanation to the Jews regarding eternal life, they couldn't hear His life-saving message over the noise of their grumbling.

In our current culture, we hear an abundance of noise about being kind and loving, but it's not for the goal of bringing glory to God. We don't show kindness because the world tells us to or because we want credit for being kind; we show kindness *out of response* to everything Christ has done for us. We do it all for Him, giving glory to God all the while.

This week, *in response to all God has done for us*, we will examine our lives and determine whether our mindset and attitude need to be transformed.

But we don't do it alone.

Prayer Points

1. God, in what areas of my life am I not responding in gratitude?

2. If you are in an open posture to God, ask Him to reveal this
for His Word says He will open your eyes. Psalm 146:8 says,
"The Lord opens the eyes of the blind. The Lord lifts up
those who are bowed down; the Lord loves the righteous."

3. How am I showing kindness to those I'm so grateful for?
How can I go above and beyond today?

4. Where do I have opportunities in my life to respond in
gratitude?

Dig Deeper

Reflect on these two verses. Pray and meditate on them today. Decide
with God which one of the two you would rather emulate:

- "He who withholds kindness from a friend forsakes the fear
of the Almighty." Job 6:14

- "Put on then, as God's chosen ones, holy and beloved,
compassionate hearts, kindness, humility, meekness, and
patience." Colossians 3:12

WEEK SIX

praise

DAY TWO

I'm feeling a shift.

"Let no corrupting talk come out of your mouths, but only such as is good for building up, as fits the occasion, that it may give grace to those who hear." Ephesians 4:29

Why it Matters:

Complaining is gratitude's nemesis.

This world is an easy place to be grouchy in. Recently, I experienced a season of grouch, which turned into a season a little darker than that. And I just wasn't okay.

Ever been there?

What it Takes:

I decided to make a simple change. I've done my absolute best to stop complaining. That's it. And I have to admit: I'm feeling a shift.

The Greek word for "unwholesome talk" used in this verse is *sapros,* which refers to "that which is foul or rotten."[21] Before your eyes glaze over at the Greek lesson, picture the impact something foul or rotten has—it stinks up the whole place and the stench spreads. Quickly. This is not the kind of language that a new life in Christ should reflect. Our life in Christ is supposed to look different than the world.

Complaining spoils moods, relationships, and hearts. It affects how we see the world and influences how others see the world.

In a recent sermon about gratitude, the pastor spoke of a friend who bought his dream car. Owning one of those old cars that men go nuts over, the new owner floated along on Cloud Nine. He enjoyed showing it off every chance he could.

One day, he spotted a scratch, just a tiny one, the kind you or I wouldn't even notice. Suddenly, the man's entire attitude changed. When others complimented it, he pointed out the scratch. He instantly stopped enjoying his dream car. Instead, he could focus only on the scratch. Focusing on the car's imperfection stole his joy.

The Israelites also mastered this. Remember when God rescued them from slavery, saved them from ten plagues, parted the Red Sea, and destroyed their enemies? Then, He gave them His ever-sought-after presence. Yet they had the nerve to "grumble against Moses and Aaron" (Ex.16:2).

How often do we forget what God has done for us?

I'm discovering that a spirit of gratitude is deeper than simply being thankful; It's being *obedient*.

"Rejoice always, pray without ceasing, give thanks in all circumstances; for this is the will of God in Christ Jesus for you." 1 Thessalonians 5:16-18

The Word tells us that God's will is for us to always rejoice, pray, and give thanks, no matter what. What it doesn't mention is the *joy this* brings. That's for us to discover on our own, even if it takes a few decades to figure it out.

I needed a shift in my mood, my marriage, my parenting, and my relationship with Christ. Keeping my mouth shut instead of complaining moved me in that direction. In turn, I didn't lash out at my kids when they acted like kids. When my husband seemed a little moody, I showed him grace. My prayers were led with gratitude.

Complaining had been holding me captive.

How to Get There:

Challenge yourself today to rid your mouth and heart of the poison of complaining. Then, take it to God in prayer so He can begin the long-lasting change your heart needs to make it stick.

I pray you feel the shift.

Prayer Points

    1. God, so much in this world isn't fair and doesn't go my way, but You are still in control. What is going on in my heart that makes me feel the need to complain rather than focus on how blessed I am?

    2. What areas in my life do I complain about the most?

    3. Lord, where do I have opportunities to shift my attitude?

Dig Deeper

Read Exodus 16. Watch their attitudes as the Israelites grumbled while God was busy providing all they needed.

WEEK SIX

praise

DAY THREE

Do I Have to *Express* Gratitude?

"I thank my God in all my remembrance of you, always in every prayer of mine for you all making my prayer with joy, because of your partnership in the gospel from the first day until now. And I am sure of this, that he who began a good work in you will bring it to completion at the day of Jesus Christ." Philippians 1:3-6

Berkeley University performed gratitude research.[22] Using college-aged people and young adults who struggled with mental health concerns and sought therapy, they gave three groups different assignments. In tandem with therapy, the first group was required to write a letter of gratitude to one person each week. The second group was assigned to write out their deepest thoughts and feelings about negative experiences in their lives. The third group did not need to do any writing activity.

Why it Matters:

The results showed that those who wrote gratitude letters reported significantly better mental health at both four weeks and twelve weeks after their writing exercise ended because they *expressed* gratitude.

Interestingly, those who wrote the letters didn't have to send them and not many did. Nevertheless, these folks had the same improvement in mental health because they *expressed* their gratitude. They shifted attention away from toxic emotions like resentment and envy to focus on nontoxic emotions.

What it Takes:

We know we live in a broken, fallen world. We can stew about it, complain about it, and be miserable. Or we can take a lesson from Paul's letter to the Philippians and choose to *express* our gratitude.

Did you know our brains change when we are grateful? At the end of the Berkeley study, actual brain scans confirmed that those who wrote gratitude letters showed distinct differences. The study concluded that simply *expressing* gratitude created lasting effects on the brain. Practicing gratitude may help train the brain to be more sensitive to the experience of gratitude. You heard that right, we can train our brain to be grateful by *expressing* our gratitude.

Remember this. They didn't all send their letters. Can you imagine what might have happened if they did?

How to Get There:

Think about how powerful we are over the people in our lives. How would our day go tomorrow morning if we woke up and told those we loved how grateful we are for them, for *who* they are? What if we told our kids our gratitude for them and then watched them light up like a Christmas tree? What impact might this have on a friend, neighbor, spouse, sister, brother, parents, or other relatives? Who are you grateful for, and why? Take time today to *express* it. Start with telling it to God in prayer.

Prayer Points

1. God, who can I express my gratitude for today?

2. In what ways can I begin to express gratitude more often?

3. What is holding me back from expressing gratitude to those who deserve it?

Dig Deeper

Paul was an affectionate soul. He expressed his gratitude toward those in letters in such a way that you can't help but feel his heart. Read through the verses listed. You won't be able to wipe the smile off your face!

Romans 1:8-12; 1 Corinthians 1:4-9; Ephesians 1:15-23; Philippians 1:3-11; Colossians 1:3-14; 1 Thess. 1:2-10; 1 Thess. 1:3-4; 2 Timothy 1:3-7; Philemon 4-7

WEEK SIX

praise

DAY FOUR

Just as Lost

"But he was angry and refused to go in. His father came out and entreated him, but he answered his father, 'Look, these many years I have served you, and I never disobeyed your command, yet you never gave me a young goat, that I might celebrate with my friends. But when this son of yours came, who has devoured your property with prostitutes, you killed the fattened calf for him'" Luke 15:28-30

Have you ever identified with the Prodigal son's older brother? Or even just understood where he was coming from? His younger brother returns home after squandering his entire inheritance, and their dad throws a grand welcome-home party. The older brother had stayed with the family and worked his tail off. *He* did what was right in the eyes of his father.

But his heart was not right. He lived entitled. In his mind, he'd earned what he had coming, and his brother deserved every bit of misery he had coming.

Why it Matters:

This story holds a deeper spiritual warning.

The prodigal's failures are showcased publicly. The older brother's hardened heart is more challenging to see, but he is just as lost as the younger brother. No one knew it, as he hid the anger well until now, but it's been festering all along. Theologian Philip Ryken explains, "Even though he had never left the family farm, he had abandoned his father's heart, and thus, he was lost in his own home."[23]

What it Takes:

Following the rules and being *good* blinded him to his own sin of entitlement and resentment. Doing the right thing for the wrong reason positions you to receive the glory instead of God getting the glory. The heart matters.

When the prodigal son returned, he expected to earn back his father's favor. He had the expectation that he would be lowered to the lowest possible position, knowing he deserved it. He came to the end of himself and came back humbled.

Grace won. His father saw his younger son and was overwhelmed with gratitude that his son had finally returned to him—overcome with joy because it was his lost but now found child. The point is that the change in the prodigal's heart was deeper.

Pastor Mason King captures it perfectly when he says, "I think all Christians are both brothers at some point in their life. We are the prodigal running from God, and we are the older, at home and offered joy and settling for duty. We can be both saved from our sin and then judge others who confess theirs. We are sinners turned saints who sin. And we are prone to distrust in the grace that made us saints. We are prone to trusting in what we can do for God over God and who He is."[24]

How to Get There:

God's expectation is our heart, all of it. His expectation reflects the grace that *is* Him. He views us through the lens of redemption: the finished work on the cross. *It is finished.* Nothing that we do can add to the grace of God. And nothing that we do can take away from it. The only work left for us is in the relationship with Him. Let your focus fall here today in open, honest prayer.

Prayer Points

1. Father, at what points in my life have I been the older brother? Where is there lingering entitlement or resentment I need to surrender to You?

2. At what points in my life have I been the prodigal? How

have I maintained that humbleness? How have I not?

3. How can I better align my heart toward gratitude for where You have placed me?

Dig Deeper

Read the story twice. Read it once through the eyes of the older brother and then again through the eyes of the prodigal.

WEEK SIX

praise

DAY FIVE

What are you seeking?

"For everything there is a season, and a time for every matter under heaven." Ecclesiastes 3:1

"So I saw that there is nothing better than that a man should rejoice in his work, for that is his lot. Who can bring him to see what will be after him?" Ecclesiastes 3:22

New seasons scare the life out of some people, but not me. I dive in blissfully unaware of the fact that things aren't going to pan out as I've so diligently planned—every single time.

Take summer break, for instance. I start the season with delightful ambitions and activities. I purchase workbooks to keep my kids' brains from melting, and plan high-protein recipes for the grill to keep us healthy and allow us to eat outside (where food always tastes better). Mid-summer finds me walking around the house wondering what will get all my time and attention: well-rounded, hardworking, hard-playing kids? A tidy, organized house that serves me well? My own mental, physical, spiritual, and emotional health? A happy, supported husband? Delicious, healthy meals?

I can't be the only one who's spun out wondering why none of my efforts ever feel like enough or why each of these areas is never perfect. And when one area thrives, the rest fall out of whack! It's the same cycle every time.

Why it Matters:

I pray for balance but secretly want perfection.

Ecclesiastes 3 says that there is a time for everything, and that God has made everything beautiful in its time. So, thinking that this season of life is not perfect enough for me is blatant disobedience to God's Word.

What it Takes:

Amid all the striving, the question remains for each of us: am I seeking perfection, or am I seeking Him?

When I start to spin out, I realize it's because I'm not surrendered to His plan. This period of time may not be what I anticipated or even what I wanted, but if God has made it beautiful in its time, then what am I even doing?

Seeking perfection steals my joy. Seeking perfection steals the blessing away from me that God has placed in front of me. I'm attempting to control when I've never been in control to begin with. There's a time to cling to plans and a time to let go. I think the time to let go is when we know God is in control.

Staring back at the summer, I recall more pizza nights than I anticipated, workbooks that collected dust, and bedtimes ignored for the sake of family movie nights and catching fireflies. God made it beautiful instead of perfect, just like the writer of Ecclesiastes said.

I need to get out of the way of perfection's pry and allow this stage of life to be exactly what God intended. As each chapter ends, you and I can rest in the words of Ecclesiastes 3:22 which says,

"So I saw that there is nothing better for a person than to enjoy their work, because that is their lot. For who can bring them to see what will happen after them."

How to Get There:

Allow God to show you what you are seeking in your heart as you open up to Him.

Prayer Points

1. Lord, You have me in this stage of life, surrounded by these people for a reason. What standard of perfection do I need to let go of?

2. How am I not honoring where You've placed me?

3. What expectations have I placed on myself that are stealing my joy?

Dig Deeper

Read Ecclesiastes 3 slowly. Reflect on the stages and seasons of your life God has brought you through with an attitude of gratefulness.

WEEK SIX

praise

DAY SIX

The Eye is the Lamp

"The eye is the lamp of the body. So, if your eye is healthy, your whole body will be full of light, but if your eye is bad, your whole body will be full of darkness. If then the light in you is darkness, how great is the darkness!" Matthew 6:22-23

The backpacks are ready, and lunches are packed. I smile and comb their hair. They brush their teeth. We all pretend it will go this seamlessly every day all year long. The highly anticipated, sometimes dreaded, first day back to school has arrived. I had the privilege of being home with my boys all summer. Man, we had fun. My kids are cool.

I often talk to moms who love being able to work and would go crazy being at home. I feel for them deeply. So much downtime may happen when you feel like you're not accomplishing anything other than losing at the game of LIFE for the 47th time or breaking up a fight. Then, some working moms would love nothing more than to be able to be home with their littles at this stage but can't.

Cue the internet.

Google "Why you should be a stay-at-home mom?" You will get 1.59 billion results.

Try instead, "Why you *shouldn't* be a stay-at-home mom?" You'll receive 2.1 billion results.

That's a lot of noise.

Why it Matters:

The world (i.e., the internet) can talk us into anything. All we must do these days is Google our problem. BOOM. A few million people will tell us what we want to hear to justify everything we're feeling. How healthy can this possibly be?

What it Takes:

God's Word tells us that we are responsible for the influence we put into our mind. What we read affects what we believe, which affects how we live.

"The eye is the lamp of the body. So, if your eye is healthy, your whole body will be full of light, but if your eye is bad, your whole body will be full of darkness. If then the light in you is darkness, how great is the darkness!" Matthew 6:22-23

Sure, this world is full of light, as the text says, but it's also full of darkness. Jesus is telling us what to do: control what our eyes see and read. If we spend every moment of our free time reading other people's opinions on life, we certainly won't be able to discern the truth when we see it.

How to Get There:

Pay attention today. How many threads do you read on social media that frustrate you? Evaluate what and who you're following. There's excellent Biblical content out there. Your heart matters so it is worth discerning whether or not that's what you indeed need to be reading. You can't afford to be vulnerable to the world's influence on your heart.

The only source of truth that has zero chance of returning void is God's truth. Dive into His Word instead of the world's noise today and see what He does. Let Him direct your eyes. Talk to Him about where your focus has been.

Prayer Points

1. God, how much of my influence is coming from the world?

2. How much influence is coming from Your Word?

3. How can I adjust my habits to remain faithful to reading your Word *before* I read other's thoughts online?

Dig Deeper

Considering all we've covered regarding gratitude, take some time with the verses below. Study, pray, and meditate on these words.

"And let the peace of Christ rule in your hearts, to which indeed you were called in one body. And be thankful. Let the word of Christ dwell in you richly, teaching and admonishing one another in all wisdom, singing psalms and hymns and spiritual songs, with thankfulness in your hearts to God. And whatever you do, in word or deed, do everything in the name of the Lord Jesus, giving thanks to God the Father through him." Colossians 3:15-17

WEEK SIX

praise

DAY SEVEN

Check-In Day

How am I praising God through a grateful attitude?

The Bible's prescription for fear and anxiety is clear:

"Do not be anxious about anything, but in everything by prayer and supplication with thanksgiving let your requests be made known to God. And the peace of God, which surpasses all understanding, will guard your hearts and your minds in Christ Jesus." Philippians 4:6-7

When my attitude gets sour, it's not always because of anxiety or fear, though it certainly may have a lot to do with it. The same part of our brains that feels these emotions can't fire simultaneously, so it has to pick one: gratitude or fear. God's Word has always known the solution. Don't be anxious, just have gratitude and pray.

We can't walk around this world saying we're Christians and we're grateful for everything while we mope around with a poor attitude. Check your attitude with God in prayer today.

Prayer Points

1. Lord, have I been adopting a grateful attitude this week?

2. How am I truly *feeling* gratitude?

3. Is something holding me back from praising You with a grateful attitude?

4. God, do I need to create a habit of gratitude to continue to make the choice to do so? In what ways will You show me how to do this?

Memorize

BELIEVE

DECIDE

SEEK

PRAY

LIVE

PRAISE

SHARE

WEEK SEVEN

Share

DAY ONE

Share Your Faith with Confidence

You've made it to the home stretch! With everything you've walked through in prayer, I can't wait for you to discover that you have all you need to share the faith you treasure deeply. Today, we take our lesson from the apostle Paul.

"Some indeed preach Christ from envy and rivalry, but others from good will. The latter do it out of love, knowing that I am put here for the defense of the Gospel." Philippians 1:15-16

Paul storms out of the gate in the first chapter of Philippians with a declaration that the believers in Philippi were partners in the Gospel (1:5). This comradery exists for a single reason: they're out to accomplish the same thing: God's plan. No agenda is placed in front of them regarding Paul's wishes or demands, just good, old-fashioned appreciation and confidence in their work. He even goes as far as to admit his desire to be in heaven with Christ, but he's content sticking around for their sake and the sake of God's purposes on this earth. Brotherly love at its finest.

Why it Matters:

In their culture, defending the Gospel presented an intimidating challenge, but Paul convincingly argues that this is their purpose. Thousands of years later, that same fear still lingers in many of us. Will I stumble with my words? Will I be mocked? Will I run out of things to say? Where do I even begin?

If our identity is in Christ, then we are also partakers in the defense of the Gospel (1:7). Intimidated or not, we are called to join the mission. However, sharing and defending our faith doesn't have to be as scary as we've made it.

What it Takes:

Apologetics—a leg of Christian theology devoted entirely to developing a defense for the Christian faith against objections—provides paths for offering Christ to others. The root of this word is borrowed from the Greek language. *Apologia* means "defense."[25] In no way does it mean we need to apologize for our Christian faith! Instead, this word aligns with developing a defense like we would see in a courtroom. Lawyers build cases based on facts, evidence, and eye-witnesses to prove a point and uphold their case. Understanding the Christian faith in this way helps us share our faith. It strengthens our faith when we logically work out some objections.

How to Get There:

Take time this week to lean into the Scripture and the devotion each day. Let God move in your heart to show you exactly how He has *already prepared* you for this important calling.

As Peter tells us in 1 Peter 3:15, "but in your hearts honor Christ the Lord as holy, always being prepared to make a defense to anyone who asks you for a reason for the hope that is in you; yet do it with gentleness and respect."

Prayer Points

1. God, as I open up to the idea of sharing my faith this week, how can I prepare myself?

2. Who are the people in my life that most need to hear my story and Yours, Lord?

3. What part of me is ashamed to talk about my faith with others?

Dig Deeper

Read Philippians 1 to clearly understand Paul's attitude in advancing the Gospel.

- In what ways do you feel as strongly as Paul did about sharing your faith?

- What hampers your enthusiasm to share your faith?

WEEK SEVEN

Share

DAY ONE

The Stories

"For God so loved the world, that he gave his only Son, that whoever believes in him should not perish but have eternal life. For God did not send his Son into the world to condemn the world, but in order that the world might be saved through him." John 3:16-17

Do you know The Story of the Gospel? Do you know what God's done for you? Do you know what He did for Abraham and Sarah, Ruth, or Paul?

We read these stories. We teach them to our kids or other people's kids. Why? Think about it. I imagine you could name a handful of reasons. We do it to learn more about God, teach kids how to live in the Kingdom of God, learn from the mistakes of those who didn't follow God, and more. The list could go on.

Why it Matters:

Recently, I learned a different perspective about this topic. It's so simple, it's refreshing.

Say I told you that I have a friend who is loyal. You'd say, "Cool!", then we'd probably just move on. Instead, what if I told you a story about the time I was in a bad spot? If I explained how everyone else in my life deserted me yet this friend stuck around. When no one else showed up, this friend poured love over me through a hard time.

Through a story, you notice their loyalty by how they acted towards me.

What it Takes:

This is exactly what happens in the Bible. Story after story introduces us to God's perfect love, justice, and mercy in the Old Testament. They all point to the Savior to come. We learn of the incredible lengths God engages in as He pursues a relationship with us. He does this for our heart. We meet Jesus. We hear everything He taught and see the sacrifice He made for our souls. We don't have to rewrite the Gospels or create something new because this truth is all we need. John 3:16 says, "For God so loved the world that he gave his one and only Son, that whoever believes in him should not perish but have eternal life."

Sometimes, we feel like we need to know more and study more about God or the Bible to become equipped to talk about Him. Yet there's a reason kids are taught by stories. Everyone loves a good story—especially ones as good as those in the Bible!

Bible stories reveal aspects of God's character. They teach who He is, One full of abundant love. People are drawn to these stories. They are attracted to *who He is*. You may understand this quite well if you've grown up on a steady diet of Bible stories. If you haven't, the good news is that you can experience them for the first time with childlike faith.

How to Get There:

Reflect today on The Story of the Gospel. Try saying it out loud from the beginning to the end of the Bible, with Jesus as the focus. If you have a hard time, commit to doing something about it using the resources below.

Prayer Points

1. God, in what ways do I experience anxiety when I talk about the Story of the Bible?

2. How can I better prepare myself to share the hope I have in the message of the Bible?

3. What can I do to build my confidence in talking about the Story of the Gospel?

Dig Deeper

Write one paragraph of the entire Story of the Bible, covering Genesis through Revelation. Then, pretend you give someone a Bible. They ask you, "Where should I start?" What 45-second explanation could you offer? Where would you have them start reading? At the beginning of Genesis? In the Book of John? Would you offer to read a book with them?

Think, pray, and wrestle with this.

Recommended Resources:

Book: *30 Days to Understanding the Bible*, Max Anders[26]

Bible Study: *Seamless*, Angie Smith[27]

Videos: *The Bible Project*, YouTube[28]

WEEK SEVEN

Share

DAY TWO

Paul

"And they have conquered him by the blood of the Lamb and by the word of their testimony, for they loved not their lives even unto death…" Revelation 12:11

Paul was a man with a dark past. As someone who previously perse-cuted Christians, he had quite the story to tell after coming to faith in God. *And he did tell it.* Paul was so enamored with what God had done through him. Yet he didn't tell it because he was proud of the evil things he'd done.

In Galatians 1:10, Paul asks simple questions to the people of Galatia,

"For am I now seeking the approval of man, or of God? Or am I trying to please man? If I were still trying to please man, I would not be a servant of Christ."

Why it Matters:

When we hesitate to share our story out of shame or regret, Paul offers his perspective. We need to pause and consider it. Who are you striving to please? Who are you serving with your reluctance, your striving?

Paul didn't hesitate. God called him, and he responded with action. I love how candidly he speaks to us:

"But when he who had set me apart before I was born, and who called me by his grace, was pleased to reveal his Son to me, in order that I might preach him among the Gentiles, I did not immediately consult with anyone." Gal 1:15-16

He wanted the approval of God, not man, so he simply took the calling and got to work.

Paul often talks of his earlier life. During his Judaism pre-conversion, he persecuted the church. He admitted he killed Christians simply because they followed Christ. Is Paul proud of what he's done? Of course not. Yet he doesn't shy away from his testimony for he knows forgiveness. The magnitude of what God did for Paul muted his shame. He says, "And they glorified God because of me." (Gal. 1:24). He let God use all his former life's story for His glory.

Shouldn't that be our goal? Revelation 12:10 b-11 talks about defeating Satan in the final days:

"for the accuser of our brothers has been thrown down, who accuses them day and night before our God. And they have conquered him by the blood of the Lamb and by the word of their testimony, for they loved not their lives even unto death."

Let us do likewise.

What it Takes:

Two weapons exist to defeat the enemy: what Jesus did on the cross and the story of what He's done for us. Influences around you may say your story is nobody's business. The enemy agrees as he spits out the lie that your story should just stay quiet in the background as that old way of living because it's nobody's business. But what would Jesus say?

Our greatest tool for sharing our faith is not winning a theological debate, knowing all the answers at Bible study, or having our lives look like we have it all together. The greatest tool we have is the same one Paul had. Share the incredible story of what God has done—a story no one else has—and with that, we have it all. What will it take for you to share the incredible love of Christ with others?

How to Get There:

Today, allow God to remind you of what He's walked through with you. This is your testimony. Reflect on your before and after story.

What were you like before you accepted the invitation to life from Jesus? What are you like now? Details regarding how "bad" or "good" you think you were before Christ are relatable to many, yes, but they aren't the star of the show. Jesus is. And the show isn't over! When you think about what a testimony is, remember it's about Christ and the redemption He has brought. Whether you think you were awful or great before He came into your life, you're wrong. None of us know the vastness of our sin and none of us can fathom the love Christ had to cover it. Tell your story, but let your testimony center on Him.

Prayer Points

1. God, who needs to hear the story of what You've done for me?

2. What have you allowed in my life that had a greater purpose in my testimony?

3. What part of my testimony will this specific person connect with?

4. How can I re-center the story of what you've done for me better around *You* instead of me?

Dig Deeper

Take time today to write out your testimony. Your first version may be long and involved. That's ok. Now revise it so you can say the whole thing in three-to-four minutes, the length of time you might have as you ride on an elevator between one floor and the next.

WEEK SEVEN

Share

DAY THREE

A Willing Testimony

"Continue steadfastly in prayer, being watchful in it with thanksgiving. At the same time, pray also for us, that God may open to us a door for the word, to declare the mystery of Christ, on account of which I am in prison—that I may make it clear, which is how I ought to speak. Walk in wisdom toward outsiders, making the best use of the time. Let your speech always be gracious, seasoned with salt, so that you may know how you ought to answer each person." Colossians 4:2-6

"Pray for your testimony more than your relief."

This gem appeared as I read over my sermon outline from Sunday. It haunted me. It goes against my normal tendencies. I'm accustomed to relief! When a pounding headache occurs, I pop some ibuprofen. When breathlessness happens during my jog, I slow the pace. When my feet hurt, I buy new, well-cushioned insoles. When I'm sad, a cry fest releases built-up emotions.

Why it Matters:

As Christians, we recognize we are called to prayer. So, when life gets tough physically, emotionally, spiritually, or otherwise, we naturally pray for relief. We ask God to remove the pain. Our gracious God often does.

But what about all those times when He doesn't offer relief? Unanswered prayers or His answer of a straight-up "no" may tempt us to be mad at God. Sometimes we just want to have it out with Him.

When we idolize relief from the pain, then we value reprieve more than we value God. The idol of comfort lures our hearts.

Yet God wants our heart.

Don't you think He deserves it? Jesus came down, walked among us, showed us how to live, to endure a burden, and tolerate pain. He understands pain.

Years ago, a friend experienced a tragedy. Mere hours after her child was born, he died. This tragedy could have shattered her faith and left her empty. Instead, she read how Jesus responded in the face of tragedy. Though my friend grieved and felt devastated, she saw Scripture with fresh eyes. A single verse met her right in the middle of her sorrow and struck her heart deeply: "Jesus wept" (John 11:35).

At that moment, she realized Jesus knew the pain she, too, was carrying. He'd wept, too.

What it Takes:

God allows us to walk in valleys of pain. Naturally, we want out of those rough valleys. Yet, sometimes, God doesn't call us out of the pain. Instead, He invites us to become a living, walking, breathing testimony. Our story shows someone who trusts God, even if relief doesn't appear. In the middle of it all, He promises to be with us always, even until the very end of the age (Matthew 28:20).

God sees the bigger picture. Though we change and grow, then fall and fail, God doesn't. He stays the same. I love that I can count on that. We all need that.

How to Get There:

Today, take your focus off this world. Let your eyes and heart land on that Kingdom mindset.

Prayer Points

1. God, this is awful, and I want You to take away the pain. I ask You to do this. But if this is what I have to bear to

give You glory, I ask You to make it big. Bring an enormous amount of good out of this.

2. How can I respond in such a way that You will receive the most glory? Give me the strength to represent You well as You work in my heart and in the hearts of others to draw them closer to You.

3. Who is it You need me to be in this situation?

4. How do I need to adjust my daily routines to ensure I'm walking with You even in the hardest of circumstances?

Dig Deeper

Read these verses. Consider what God has allowed you to walk through and what His purpose has been for you.

- "But he said to me, 'My grace is sufficient for you, for my power is made perfect in weakness.' Therefore I will boast all the more gladly of my weaknesses, so that the power of Christ may rest upon me." 2 Corin, 12:9

- "For I consider that the sufferings of this present time are not worth comparing with the glory that is to be revealed to us." Romans 8:18

- "Not only that, but we rejoice in our sufferings, knowing that suffering produces endurance; and endurance produces character; and character produces hope, and hope does not put us to shame, because God's love has been poured out into our hearts through the Holy Spirit, who has been given to us." Romans 5:3-5

WEEK SEVEN

Share

DAY FIVE

The Invitation

"I appeal to you therefore, brothers, by the mercies of God, to present your bodies as a living sacrifice, holy and acceptable to God, which is your spiritual worship." Romans 12:1

I've been reminded this past week of the invitation we have from Jesus to be in relationship with Him.

The invitation.

Not the demand, not the requirement, but the invitation.

In this text, Paul doesn't command. He says, "I urge you." The Greek word he uses here is *parakaleo*, which means "to invite, call near, or be of good comfort."[29] The way you and I understand the word "urge" is a bit pushier. Instead, this is an excited invitation—not a pressured forcing, but an invitation.

Doesn't that reflect the entire Gospel message? This is the true invitation from Christ. An invitation is a choice. You have a choice. You can choose to keep on carrying the weight you are carrying, as you live in the world's way. God does not force you to follow Him. It's an invitation, not a demand.

Why it Matters:

I can't help but think of those I care about who aren't in relationship with God. How I long for them to experience the love of Christ! I want them to experience what's possible. To walk in the freedom of knowing their life is in His hands. To find joy in Him when this world fails to offer joy. To know forever is taken care of as He wants us with Him.

I want this for them desperately, but I can't force it because God doesn't force it. He loves us enough to let us choose—to walk with Him on this earth and with Him in heaven. Or don't.

God gives us a very specific invitation and we're allowed to say no. Our loved ones are allowed to say no, too.

What it Takes:

Here's the question we must ask: Do we love our *relationship* with people more than we love them? Might it worth putting our relationship on the line to bear a little awkwardness for the sake of their soul?

What if we give them a Bible? What if we simply say, "I love you. I don't want you to miss out on something that I have that has been *everything* to me!" Then, we storm the gates of heaven with prayer.

Rather than spewing our faith in their face in an obnoxious manner, let's choose *parakaleo*. Let's "invite" and "excitedly offer" them the opportunity to know Christ. Let's love them to Jesus.

Well-known atheist Penn Jillette (of Penn and Teller) says this:

"I've always said that I don't respect people who don't proselytize (which means to preach, evangelize). I don't respect that at all. If you believe that there's a heaven and a hell, and people could be going to hell or not getting eternal life, and you think that it's not really worth telling them this because it would make it socially awkward—and atheists who think people shouldn't proselytize and who say just leave me alone and keep your religion to yourself—how much do you have to hate somebody to not proselytize? How much do you have to hate somebody to believe everlasting life is possible and not tell them that? I mean, if I believed, beyond the shadow of a doubt, that a truck was coming at you, and you didn't believe that truck was bearing down on you, there is a certain point where I tackle you. And this is more important than that."[30]

Even a man who doesn't believe in God sees the importance of sharing faith with others if the person is truly that important to you.

Keep praying for the people who you want to see come to a life with Christ. If you haven't already done so, I challenge you to do something with your hopes. Pray and ask God for opportunities. Invite them to church because they just may say yes.

Do you love the relationship more than you love the person? Don't let them miss the greatest gift in all of eternity.

How to Get There:

Spend intentional time in prayer today about the person you want to reach.

Prayer Points

1. Who is it, Lord? Who is the person You have placed in my life?

2. What can I do today or this week to share my hope in You?

3. How have You prepared me to share the truth of the Gospel with them?

Dig Deeper

Read 1 Peter 3:15. Christian apologists, people who have studied and researched how to effectively share the Christian faith with gentleness and respect, have an abundance of resources available. Check out these Christian apologists: Alisa Childers[31], Natasha Crain[32],

Greg Koukl[33], Mama Bear Apologetics[34], Sean McDowell[35], Frank Turek[36], J. Warner Wallace[37].

WEEK SEVEN

Share

DAY SIX

Joy

"I thank my God in all my remembrance of you, always in every prayer of mine for you all making my prayer with joy, because of your partnership in the gospel from the first day until now. And I am sure of this, that he who began a good work in you will bring it to completion at the day of Jesus Christ." Philippians 1:3-6

Philippians is the go-to book of the Bible on joy. Yet, on the surface, it doesn't seem as though Paul set out for joy to be the topic. It doesn't seem like he was *trying* to instill joy in the people of Philippi. He's not *trying* to choose joy or telling them to do so. The joy Paul possesses can't be locked down or taught; it's pouring out of his soul.

Why It Matters:

He's in jail, and jail isn't fun. Still, there's this joy he speaks of, a deep, pure joy that trickles into every line of the book. His joy doesn't come from health, finances, or perfect relationships. He's not looking for it in these things, so he's not finding it in these things. As he speaks, he initially shares his thankfulness and gives godly wisdom. Then, he focuses on warning the people at Philippi of the threat of persecution that could be headed toward them.

Anyone else might sound more upset, but not our Paul. He prays with joy for the following reasons in Philippians:

"because of your sharing in the Gospel from the first day until

Now" (1:5)

"that the one who began a good work among you will bring it to

completion by the day of Jesus Christ" (1:6)

"for all of you share in God's grace with me, both in my

imprisonment and in the defense and confirmation of the

gospel." (1:7)

[that you will] "produce a harvest of righteousness that comes

through Jesus Christ for the glory and praise of God" (1:11)

"what has happened to me has actually helped to spread the

gospel"(1:12)

"And because of my chains, most of the brothers and sisters have become confident in the Lord and dare all the more to proclaim the gospel without fear." (1:14)

What It Takes:

Circumstances need not shake us. Joy seeps out of Paul's soul onto the pages of this book because of Jesus. Paul is in jail, yet he's rejoicing because it has served to advance the Gospel. As long as people meet Jesus, Paul's good with what's happening in his life.

How To Get There:

When we talk about our faith and feel intimidation creep in, this is where we can turn. In moments when our tongue slips, we say the wrong thing, or we're stumped about which direction to head in the conversation, we remember that Jesus is our joy. He is the Father's joy.

Our joy is in what Jesus did for us, in the gift we have of the Holy Spirit, in our Father in heaven always watching over us, and in the fact that we can share our reason for joy without the threat of being thrown in jail. And even if we do end up like Paul, our joy is in the trust we have that God put us there for the grand purpose of spreading the Good News—the joy that is in Christ.

We are partakers in spreading the Gospel (Phil 1:5). Instead of this truth landing on our shoulders as one more thing we ought to do that scares us, let's lean into the joy it offers.

Our witness can be as simple as saying, "There's a joy I've found in Christ unlike anything else I've found on this planet."

Take time for honest prayer today. Ask God to reveal how much stock you put in circumstances, whether it hinders the joy He has provided for you, and, thus, has hindered your witness.

Prayer Points

1. God, how much focus do I put on my circumstances? How do I let circumstances control my mood and my mindset?

2. How am I finding joy in You? How am I looking for it in other things?

3. What do nonbelievers see in me that is different? Is the joy from my spirit pouring out?

Dig Deeper

Read all four chapters of Philippians. Notice the tone of the language and Paul's attitude toward advancing the Gospel.

WEEK SEVEN

Share

DAY SEVEN

Check-In

How has God equipped me to share my faith with confidence?

The God we serve never leaves us to fend for ourselves. He equips those He calls. As we read in Philippians, we are all partners in sharing the Gospel (Phil 1:5). That means He has called each of us to share the faith He gave us with others.

Today, let your thoughts fall on all that God has done to prepare you for this important call on your life. Hopefully, this calling is not as intimidating as it was a week ago. You know the Gospel story; you know the story of what God has done for you. You know the joy a relationship with Christ offers. Don't keep it to yourself! Now is your chance to love the people God has placed in your life well by offering them the hope you have in Jesus Christ.

Remember that your testimony is about Him. It's about what He's done. Your testimony is not a summary of all the terrible things that have happened or all the good things that have happened. It's about *what He's done*. Don't overcomplicate it, simply let Him shine through.

Prayer Points

1. How can I open the conversation with the person in my life with whom I have the strongest desire to share my faith?

2. Lord, what are some additional things you've walked me through that haven't come to mind yet?

3. What have you taught me these seven weeks that I can take into future conversations about my faith?

Conclusion

C ONCLUSION IS AN INAPPROPRIATE title because this is only
the beginning of your renewed prayer life with God. Let's
recall what we've walked through with God these last seven weeks.
Week by week, we've investigated ways to transform your life by
changing your prayer habits.

Once you have chosen to BELIEVE in God's perfect providence,
this solid foundation allows you to DECIDE to let Him lead. You
can only follow His lead when you SEEK His voice by honoring
Scripture. You respond to His voice and stay in close relationship
with Him when you PRAY like your life depends on it. Through
this relationship, He teaches you to LIVE life God's way and in
response to all He is and all He's done, you PRAISE God through a
grateful attitude. Then, you become a living, breathing testimony of
all He has done in you, and you SHARE your faith with confidence,
knowing He will use it for His glory.

This process takes *attention*, not work, not striving, but daily surrender. With all the love in my heart, I will tell you that it requires you
to get over yourself, as you venture out into the self-obsessed nature
of this world. Remember: it's not about you; it's about Him. Trust
me, it's a much better way.

My prayer is that God has begun to teach you how to pray like your life depends on it because trust me, it does. These seven steps now represent something you can take with you. Use them to pray through when life hits hard with big and small situations alike.

For instance, recently we received some scary medical news in our family. Before I even began to process the information, I went for a walk. That gave me time to pray through these seven steps, inviting God in. It sounded something like this:

"Lord, no matter my feelings now, I want to trust and **BELIEVE** in You and Your perfect providence. Show me how to trust when it's hard, and help me remember all that You are, all You've done already, and all You're capable of. I will **DECIDE** right now to let you lead, but since I'm pretty much helpless in this situation, I only ask You, 'Who do you need me to be through this?' I ask You to speak to me through Your Word as I **SEEK** You in it. I commit to **PRAY** daily, intentionally and honestly. Lead me to **LIVE** life Your way, not mine. Show me how to **PRAISE** You with a grateful attitude through this. And no matter what, allow me to be a living, walking, breathing testimony of Your love and goodness through it all and be able to **SHARE** everything You've done ."

This way of prayer exemplifies how to go through life with God. It keeps us accountable, reminds us of our role and our priorities, retrains our heart to turn in His direction, and challenges us to live a life that brings Him glory.

God is nowhere near done with you or me. We constantly need His grace. With this kind of prayerfulness, life becomes calmer and less exhausting that the one we created before discovering this path.

Before we react, we go to God. We invite Him in before we start to process any news, good or bad. Then He accompanies us as we journey onwards in this world, but *we see His victory—**our testimony** of what He is going to do with this situation* before we even begin to process anything. Keeping our gaze on God, we trust and surrender to Him, so He receives the glory.

Consider the lengths God has gone to call us to Himself, to be in relationship with us. The Tabernacle was built in the Old Testament because He desperately wanted to dwell among His people. Then, He sent His Son, the Son that had been with Him eternally, to teach us how to live and love well and to die so our sins would be taken care of, and then to rise again to bring us to Himself and achieve everything the Bible predicted. Then, we received the Holy Spirit to continue that relationship with God, Him dwelling inside us.

It's *our* job to rest in the finished work of Christ and to remember how far He has gone to be with us. He wants us to bring our whole heart to Him, not just half of it, not just coming to Him when we are all cleaned up. He wants the truth that's within us. He has enough grace to cover it all. He has the power to transform our hearts. He longs to overcome these sinful areas in our lives one at a time when we present it all to Him. Slowly, one by one, He works in each area, preventing regret and shame. We can genuinely live in freedom from our weaknesses by His transforming love.

Here's what strikes me the most: **He *wants* our heart.**

He doesn't *need* it. God is perfectly fulfilled within the Trinity. He didn't create you and me to fulfill Him; He made us out of love for us. We don't need to help Him out with anything. Let that go. He doesn't *need* your heart. He *wants* it. He *desires* it.

He doesn't need you to go through the motions of Christian-type things or stare at a Bible study just so you can say you did it. He doesn't need you to *do* solely for the sake of doing.

He wants to go into those areas of sin and free you from them, but He doesn't force it. Yet, when we hold onto these sins, one by one, they tighten the grip until *we* can't breathe. By surrendering these areas in our lives, one by one, *He* gives us freedom (Gal. 5:1).

He loves you more than anyone else on this planet ever will.

May you use these steps to open your heart to Him; He's ready for you. I'll be here, praying for you.

"The grace of the Lord Jesus be with your spirit." Philippians 4:23

Acknowledgments

WHILE THIS BOOK STARTED as a simple project to pull to-gether a handful of teachings and devotions, God had some-thing else in mind. He blew me away. Lord, how grateful I am to be along for the ride. My heart is full.

Dr. John Coe, many of the overarching theological concepts were derived from your mind and your teachings offered at Biola University's Talbot School of Theology. Your "Spiritual Formation" course changed my prayer life and, thus, my relationship with Christ in more ways than I can explain. This book shows how God brought many of your class lessons to life. God indeed did a work in my heart, "cracked it open," as you would say, and allowed me to be a living, breathing, walking testimony. I hope I did it justice, Sir!

My hubby and boys are my world and have been such champs in this process. Thank you to my sweet little family for your love, support, ideas, and encouragement. I love you more every day.

My folks, in-laws, and grandparents: Your godly example to our family stands as your legacy. I am so grateful for each of you.

My beta readers: I asked you because I trust and respect you. Thank you for saying yes and spending the time to read my heart on the page.

My Power Hour crew: You have taught me so much over the years and brought out something in me I didn't know was within me. Thank you for your invaluable friendships, encouragement, and love.

Bethany: Everything you touch, you make beautiful! Thank you for using your gift for the glory of God. I could stare at the cover for hours!

Pastor Brad: I value your opinion. Thank you for taking the time to ensure that my heart and theology align.

Lane Arnold: You took a hot mess of a manuscript. Then you nudged me along, page by page. You polished the rough draft until it became exactly what God set it out to be. I am so grateful for your book coaching and editorial skills and your heart and work as a spiritual director that offered wisdom.

I am blessed with many godly men and women who continue to pour into my soul. Thank you for each and every nugget of love. Keep pointing me to Him.

Notes

I NTRODUCTION

1. Dr. John Coe, "Spiritual Formation 1" (Talbot School of Theology, Biola University in La Mirada, CA, 2023), Module 4, Lecture 1.

Chapter 1: BELIEVE

1. Unless otherwise noted, all Scripture used is in the ESV.

2. The Greek word for providence is *pronoia* and it is mentioned once in Acts 24:2 in reference to human providence, not Divine providence.

Chapter 2: DECIDE

1. John Piper, "What does it mean to live in the flesh", Desiring God, (2019), accessed May 24, 2024, https://www.desiringgod.org/interviews/what-does-it-mean-to-live-in-the-flesh.

2. Dr. John Coe, "Types of Spiritual Formation and Christ-

ian Spiritual Formation" (Talbot School of Theology, Biola University, La Mirada, CA, 2023), Module 1, pages 1-2.

3. R.C. Sproul, "The Glory of God and the Glory of Man," (2020), Ligonier Ministries, accessed April 14, 2024, https://www.ligonier.org/learn/articles/glory-man-and-glory-god?srsltid=AfmBOooU8vKt2Q-m-cQtmTrFfy3wChN36R8DTBpgIgnC53XXrJE63yKV.

4. Laura Story, *When God Doesn't Fix It: Lessons You Never Wanted to Learn, Truths You Can't Live Without* (Nashville: Thomas Nelson, 2015), 142.

5. Norman L. Geisler, *Chosen But Free: A Balanced View of God's Sovereignty and Free Will* (Ada, Bethany House Publishers, 1999).

Chapter 3: SEEK

1. Walter B. Russell III, Ph. D, "Is Genre Sensitivity Really Necessary in Preaching and Teaching the Bible?" (Talbot School of Theology, 2021), 2.

2. *NIV Study Bible Commentary* (Grand Rapids, Zondervan, 2011), 952.

Chapter 4: PRAY

1. Kyle Strobel and John Coe, *Where Prayer Becomes Real: How Honesty With God Transforms Your Soul,* (Ada: Baker

Books, 2021), back cover.

2. This was a repeated question in the Spiritual Formation course and asked in multiple ways in various forums and lectures.

3. Max Lucado, *"Max on Life: Discovering the Power of Prayer,"* (New York City: Harper Collins, 2007), 9.

4. Dr. John H. Coe, *Prayer of Intentions* (John H. Coe, La Mirada, © copyright 2006).

Chapter 5: LIVE

1. James Montgomery Boice, *Foundations of the Christian Faith*, (InterVarsity Press, 1986), 674.

2. C.S. Lewis, *Mere Christianity* (London, England: Geoffrey Bles, © copyright 1942, 1943, 1944, 1952 C.S. Lewis Pte. Ltd.), 15. Extracts reprinted by permission.

3. James Strong, *The New Strong's Exhaustive Concordance of the Bible,* (Nashville, Thomas Nelson, ©1995), 98,

4. Bill Gaultiere, *Jesus Set Boundaries*, accessed on January 2, 2022, https://www.soulshepherding.org/jesus-set-bound aries.

5. C.S. Lewis, *Undeceptions*(Geoffrey Bles, London, © copyright 1971 C.S. Lewis Pte. Ltd.), pp. 233-7. Extracts reprinted by permission.

6. *Merriam Webster Dictionary*, 2013. (Springfield), 405.

Chapter 6: PRAISE

1. Strong, *The New Strong's Exhaustive Concordance of the Bible*, (Nashville, Thomas Nelson, ©1995),80.

2. Greater Good Science Center at Berkeley University, *How Gratitude Changes You and Your Brain*, (2020), accessed 2020, https://greatergood.berkeley.edu/article/item/how_gratitude_changes_you_and_your_brain.

3. Philip Graham Ryken, *Luke Volume 2 – Reformed Expository Commentary* (Phillipsburg, New Jersey, 2009), Luke Chapter 15.

4. "Lost at Home," YouTube video, posted by The Village Church/Pastor Mason King, November 19, 2023: https://www.youtube.com/watch?v=-mixb66lvQE.

Chapter 7: SHARE

1. Strong, *The New Strong's Exhaustive Concordance of the Bible*, (Nashville, Thomas Nelson, ©1995), 11.

2. Max Anders, *30 Days to Understanding the Bible: Unlock the Scriptures in 15 Minutes a day[LA2]* [AR3] (Nashville, Thomas Nelson, 2018[LA4]).

3. Angie Smith, *Seamless Bible Study* ((Nashville, Lifeway

Press ©2015).

4. The Bible Project: www.thebibleproject.com or search on Youtube.

5. Strong, *The New Strong's Exhaustive Concordance of the Bible*, (Nashville, Thomas Nelson. ©1995), 67.

6. "Not Proselytize," YouTube video of Penn Jillette, posted by Rich Maurer, November 13, 2009, https://youtu.be/o wZc3Xq8obk.

7. Alisa Childers: www.alisachilders.com

8. Natasha Crain: www.natashacrain.com

9. Greg Koukl: www.str.orghttp://www.str.org (Stand to Reason Ministries)

10. Mama Bear Apologetics: www.mamabearapologetics.com

11. Sean McDowell: www.seanmcdowell.org

12. Frank Turek: www.crossexamined.org

13. J. Warner Wallace: www.coldcasechristianity.com

Author Bio

ANDI RISPENS IS A wife, mom to two boys, and lifelong learner. She is pursuing a Master of Arts degree in Bible Exposition from Biola University. She has been teaching and leading Bible studies since 2016. Since 2020, she develops concepts and content for yearly women's retreats which she leads. Her passions include women's discipleship and reading the Bible the way it was intended!

Follow: Andi Rispens Author/Speaker on Facebook or go to www.andirispens.com.

Contact: info@andirispens.com

Additional copies of this book are available to order on Amazon.com.

1. Dr. John Coe, "Spiritual Formation 1" (Talbot School of Theology, Biola University in La Mirada, CA, 2023), Module 4, Lecture 1.

2. Unless otherwise noted, all Scripture used is in the ESV.

3. The Greek word for providence is *pronoia* and it is mentioned once in Acts 24:2 in reference to human providence, not Divine providence.

4. John Piper, "What does it mean to live in the flesh", Desiring God, (2019), accessed May 24, 2024, https://www.desiringgod.org/interviews/what-does-it-mean-to-live-in-the-flesh.

5. Dr. John Coe, "Types of Spiritual Formation and Christian Spiritual Formation" (Talbot School of Theology, Biola University, La Mirada, CA, 2023), Module 1, pages 1-2.

6. R.C. Sproul, "The Glory of God and the Glory of Man," (2020), Ligonier Ministries, accessed April 14, 2024, https://www.ligonier.org/learn/articles/glory-man-and-glory-god?srsltid=AfmBOooU8vKt2Q-m-cQtmTrFfy3wChN36R8DTBpgIgnC53XXrJE63yKV.

7. Laura Story, *When God Doesn't Fix It: Lessons You Never Wanted to Learn, Truths You Can't Live Without* (Nashville: Thomas Nelson, 2015), 142.

8. Norman L. Geisler, *Chosen But Free: A Balanced View of God's Sovereignty and Free Will* (Ada, Bethany House Publishers, 1999).

9. Walter B. Russell III, Ph. D, "Is Genre Sensitivity Really Necessary in Preaching and Teaching the Bible?" (Talbot School of Theology, 2021), 2.

10. *NIV Study Bible Commentary* (Grand Rapids, Zondervan, 2011), 952.

11. Kyle Strobel and John Coe, *Where Prayer Becomes Real: How Honesty With God Transforms Your Soul,* (Ada: Baker Books, 2021), back cover.

12. This was a repeated question in the Spiritual Formation course and asked in multiple ways in various forums and lectures.

13. Max Lucado, *"Max on Life: Discovering the Power of Prayer,"* (New York City: Harper Collins, 2007), 9.

14. Dr. John H. Coe, *Prayer of Intentions* (John H. Coe, La Mirada, © copyright 2006).

15. James Montgomery Boice, *Foundations of the Christian Faith,* (InterVarsity Press, 1986), 674.

16. C.S. Lewis, *Mere Christianity* (London, England: Geoffrey Bles, © copyright 1942, 1943, 1944, 1952 C.S. Lewis Pte. L td.), 15. Extracts reprinted by permission.

17. James Strong, *The New Strong's Exhaustive Concordance of the Bible,* (Nashville, Thomas Nelson, ©1995), 98.

18. Bill Gaultiere, *Jesus Set Boundaries,* accessed on January 2, 2022, https://www.soulshepherding.org/jesus-set-boundaries.

19. C.S. Lewis, *Undeceptions* (Geoffrey Bles, London, © copyright 1971 C.S. Lewis Pte. Ltd.), pp. 233-7. Extracts reprinted by permission.

20. *Merriam Webster Dictionary*, 2013. (Springfield), 405.

21. Strong, *The New Strong's Exhaustive Concordance of the Bible*, (Nashville, Thomas Nelson, ©1995), 80.

22. Greater Good Science Center at Berkeley University, *How Gratitude Changes You and Your Brain*, (2020), accessed 2020, https://greatergood.berkeley.edu/article/item/how_gr atitude_changes_you_and_your_brain.

23. Philip Graham Ryken, Luke, ed. Richard D. Phillips, Philip Graham Ryken, and Daniel M. Doriani, vol. 2, Reformed Expository Commentary (Phillipsburg, NJ: P&R Publishing, 2009), 154.

24. "Lost at Home," YouTube video, posted by The Village Church/Pastor Mason King, November 19, 2023: https://w ww.youtube.com/watch?v=-mixb66lvQE.

25. Strong, *The New Strong's Exhaustive Concordance of the Bible*, (Nashville, Thomas Nelson, ©1995), 11.

26. Max Anders, *30 Days to Understanding the Bible: Unlock the Scriptures in 15 Minutes a day* (Nashville, Thomas Nelson, 2018).

27. Angie Smith, *Seamless Bible Study* ((Nashville, Lifeway Press ©2015).

230

28. The Bible Project: www.thebibleproject.com or search on Youtube.

29. Strong, *The New Strong's Exhaustive Concordance of the Bible*, (Nashville, Thomas Nelson, ©1995), 67.

30. "Not Proselytize," YouTube video of Penn Jillette, posted by Rich Maurer, November 13, 2009, https://youtu.be/owZc3 Xq8obk.

31. Alisa Childers: www.alisachilders.com

32. www.natashacrain.com

33. www.str.org

34. www.mamabearapologetics.com

35. www.seanmcdowell.org

36. www.crossexamined.org

37. www.coldcasechristianity.com